First World War
and Army of Occupation
War Diary
France, Belgium and Germany

37 DIVISION
Divisional Troops
Machine Gun Corps
37 Battalion
4 March 1918 - 31 May 1919

WO95/2524/3

The Naval & Military Press Ltd
www.nmarchive.com
Published in association with The National Archives

Published by

The Naval & Military Press Ltd

Unit 10 Ridgewood Industrial Park,
Uckfield, East Sussex,
TN22 5QE England
Tel: +44 (0) 1825 749494

www.naval-military-press.com
www.nmarchive.com

This diary has been reprinted in facsimile from the original. Any imperfections are inevitably reproduced and the quality may fall short of modern type and cartographic standards.

© **Crown Copyright**
Images reproduced by permission of The National Archives, London, England, 2015.

Contents

Document type	Place/Title	Date From	Date To
Heading	WO95/2524/2 37 Btn Machine Gun Corps March 1918-March 1919		
Heading	BEF 37 Div Troops 37 Bn M.G. Corps 1918 Mar-1919 Mar		
War Diary	Bristol Camp Dickebusch Area	04/03/1918	04/03/1918
War Diary	Bristol Camp (BHQ) & Line	05/03/1918	19/03/1918
War Diary	Line & Bristol Camp, Nr Dickebusch Belgium	20/03/1918	31/03/1918
Miscellaneous	Special Report on Operations (M/G) on Left Sector. by Lt H.G. Stearns O.C. "D" Coy Advd H.Q. In the Field.	09/03/1918	09/03/1918
Heading	IV. Corps. War Diary 37th Battalion, Machine Gun Corps. April 1918		
War Diary	Marieux Authie Grenas.	01/04/1918	01/04/1918
War Diary	Hebuterne Div. Sector	02/04/1918	18/04/1918
War Diary	Authie Wood	18/04/1918	18/04/1918
War Diary	Bois Du Warnimont	19/04/1918	24/04/1918
War Diary	Bucquoy Sector	25/04/1918	30/04/1918
Heading	Operation Orders.		
Operation(al) Order(s)	Operations Orders No 20 by Lieut Colonel W.V.L Prescott-Westear Cmdg 37th Bn M.G.C.		
Miscellaneous	Operations Orders No 21 by Lieut Col W.V.L. Prescott-Westear DSO Commanding 37th Bn Machine Gun Corps.	12/04/1918	12/04/1918
Operation(al) Order(s)	Operations Orders No. 22 by Lieut-Colonel W.V.L. Prescott-Westear DSO Cmdg 37th Bn M.G.C.	03/04/1918	03/04/1918
Operation(al) Order(s)	Operations Orders No. 24 by Lt. Col W.V.L. Prescott-Westear DSO Cmdg 37th Bn Machine Gun Corps	08/04/1918	08/04/1918
Operation(al) Order(s)	Operation Order No. 23 37th Divisional Order No 187	06/04/1918	06/04/1918
Operation(al) Order(s)	Revised Appendix to Operation Order No 24 by Lieut Colonel W.V.L. Prescott-Westear D.S.O. Cmdg 37th Bn Machine Gun Corps.	08/04/1918	08/04/1918
Operation(al) Order(s)	Appendix to Operation Order No. 24 By Lieut-Colonel. W.V.L. Prescott-Westear, D.S.O. Cmdg 37th Bn Machine Gun Corps	08/04/1918	08/04/1918
Operation(al) Order(s)	Amendment to Operation Order No. 24 of 8-4-18 by Lieut-Col. W.V.L. Prescott-Westear, D.S.O. Cmdg 37th Bn Machine Gun Corps	08/04/1918	08/04/1918
Operation(al) Order(s)	Amendment to Operation Order No. 24 of 8-4-18 by Lieut-Colonel. W.V.L. Prescott-Westear, D.S.O. Cmdg 37th Bn Machine Gun Corps	09/04/1918	09/04/1918
Operation(al) Order(s)	Operation Order No. 25 by Lieut-Colonel. W.V.L. Prescott-Westear, D.S.O. Cmdg 37th Bn Machine Gun Corps	12/04/1918	12/04/1918
Operation(al) Order(s)	Operation Order No. 26 by Lieut-Colonel. W.V.L. Prescott-Westear. D.S.O. Commanding 37th Bn Machine Gun Corps	15/04/1918	15/04/1918
Operation(al) Order(s)	Operation Order No. 27 by Lieut-Colonel. W.V.L. Prescott-Westear, D.S.O. Commanding 37th Bn Machine Gun Corps	23/04/1918	23/04/1918
Heading	Tracings.		
Diagram etc	Gun Position as Taken over from 62nd Bn. M.G.C.		

Map	Target Map 7.4.18		
Map	Gun Positions After Re-Grouping. 8.4.18		
Miscellaneous	Gun Positions After Re-Grouping. 8.4.18		
Map			
Map	Sheet 57D NE		
War Diary	Bucquoy Sector	01/05/1918	17/05/1918
War Diary	Henu	17/05/1918	17/05/1918
War Diary	Authie	17/05/1918	17/05/1918
War Diary	Bucquoy Sector.	18/05/1918	18/05/1918
War Diary	Bois Du. Warnimont.	18/05/1918	19/05/1918
War Diary	Orville	19/05/1918	19/05/1918
War Diary	Bois Du Warnimont.	19/05/1918	20/05/1918
War Diary	Orville	20/05/1918	20/05/1918
War Diary	Bois Du Warnimont.	21/05/1918	21/05/1918
War Diary	Orville	21/05/1918	21/05/1918
War Diary	Bois Du Warnimont	22/05/1918	22/05/1918
War Diary	Orville	22/05/1918	22/05/1918
War Diary	Bois du Warnimont	23/05/1918	23/05/1918
War Diary	Orville	23/05/1918	23/05/1918
War Diary	Bois Du Warnimont	24/05/1918	24/05/1918
War Diary	Orville	24/05/1918	24/05/1918
War Diary	Bois Du Warnimont	25/05/1918	25/05/1918
War Diary	Orville	25/05/1918	25/05/1918
War Diary	Sailly au Bois Sector	25/05/1918	26/05/1918
War Diary	Bois Du Warnimont	26/05/1918	26/05/1918
War Diary	Orville	26/05/1918	26/05/1918
War Diary	Sailly au Bois	27/05/1918	27/05/1918
War Diary	Orville	27/05/1918	27/05/1918
War Diary	Bois Du Warnimont	27/05/1918	28/05/1918
War Diary	Orville	28/05/1918	28/05/1918
War Diary	Sailly Au Bois.	28/05/1918	29/05/1918
War Diary	Orville	29/05/1918	29/05/1918
War Diary	Bois Du Warnimont	29/05/1918	29/05/1918
War Diary	Sailly Au Bois	30/05/1918	30/05/1918
War Diary	Orville	30/05/1918	30/05/1918
War Diary	Bois Du Warnimont	30/05/1918	30/05/1918
War Diary	Sailly au Bois	31/05/1918	31/05/1918
War Diary	Bois Du Warnimont	31/05/1918	31/05/1918
War Diary	Orville	31/05/1918	31/05/1918
Miscellaneous			
Operation(al) Order(s)	37th Battalion Machine Gun Corps. Operation Order No 28. Appendix 1	15/05/1918	15/05/1918
Operation(al) Order(s)	37th Battalion Machine Gun Corps. Operation Order No 29. Appendix II	22/05/1918	22/05/1918
Operation(al) Order(s)	37th Battalion Machine Gun Corps. Operation Order No 30. Appendix III	24/05/1918	24/05/1918
Operation(al) Order(s)	37th Battalion Machine Gun Corps. Operation Order No 32. Appendix V	29/05/1918	29/05/1918
Operation(al) Order(s)	37th Battalion Machine Gun Corps. Operation Order No 31. Appendix IV	26/05/1918	26/05/1918
Heading	37th Battalion Machine Gun Corps War Diary month of June 1918. Vol 4		
War Diary	Bois du Warnimont.	01/06/1918	01/06/1918
War Diary	Orville	01/06/1918	01/06/1918
War Diary	Sailly au Bois Sector	01/06/1918	01/06/1918
War Diary	Bois Du Warnimont	02/06/1918	02/06/1918

War Diary	Orville	02/06/1918	02/06/1918
War Diary	Sailly au Bois	02/06/1918	04/06/1918
War Diary	Bois Du Warnimont	05/06/1918	05/06/1918
War Diary	Cavillon Area	06/06/1918	09/06/1918
War Diary	Conoy Area	10/06/1918	18/06/1918
War Diary	Conty Area	19/06/1918	21/06/1918
War Diary	Pas Area	22/06/1918	23/06/1918
War Diary	Bucquoy Sector	24/06/1918	30/06/1918
Operation(al) Order(s)	37th Battalion. Machine Gun Corps. Operation Order No. 33. Appendix I	31/05/1918	31/05/1918
Operation(al) Order(s)	37th Battalion, Machine Gun Corps. Order No. 34. Appendix II	06/06/1918	06/06/1918
Operation(al) Order(s)	37th Battalion, M.G. Corps Operation Order No. 35. Appendix III	10/06/1918	10/06/1918
Operation(al) Order(s)	37th Bn. Machine Gun Corps Order No. 38. Appendix V	22/06/1918	22/06/1918
Operation(al) Order(s)	37th Battn. M.G. Corps. Operation Order No. 36. Appendix IV.	14/06/1918	14/06/1918
Operation(al) Order(s)	Amendment to amendment to 37th Bn M.G. Corps Order No. 38.	23/06/1918	23/06/1918
Miscellaneous	M.G. 181. Appendix VI	28/06/1918	28/06/1918
Heading	37th Bn Machine Gun Corps War Diary for the month of July 1918 Vol 5		
War Diary	Bucquoy Sector.	01/07/1918	31/07/1918
Miscellaneous			
Operation(al) Order(s)	37th Battalion. Machine Gun Corps. Order No. 39 Appendix 1	01/07/1918	01/07/1918
Operation(al) Order(s)	37th Battalion. Machine Gun Corps. Order No. 40 Appendix 2	02/07/1918	02/07/1918
Map	Dispositions of M.G's. in 37th Div Sector Super-impose on Sheet 57D N.E.		
Diagram etc	Superimpose on Sheet 57D N.E. 1:20,000		
Operation(al) Order(s)	37th Battalion, Machine Gun Corps. Operation Order No. 41. Appendix 3	11/07/1918	11/07/1918
Miscellaneous	C Coy. 37th Bn. M.G.C. Appendix 4	18/07/1918	18/07/1918
Operation(al) Order(s)	27th Battalion Machine Gun Corps. Operation Order No.42. Appendix 5	22/07/1918	22/07/1918
Operation(al) Order(s)	37th Batt' Machine Gun Corps. Operation Order No. 43 Appendix 6	23/07/1918	23/07/1918
Operation(al) Order(s)	37th Battalion Machine Gun Corps. Operation Order No. 44. Appendix 7	29/07/1918	29/07/1918
Heading	37th Bn M.G.C. War Diary for month of August 1918. Vol 6		
War Diary	Bucquoy Sector	01/08/1918	31/08/1918
War Diary	27th Battalion Machine Gun Corps. Operation Order No. 43. Appendix 1	02/08/1918	02/08/1918
Operation(al) Order(s)	37th Battalion Machine Gun Corps. Operation Order No. 46. Appendix 2	11/08/1918	11/08/1918
Operation(al) Order(s)	27th Battalion Machine Gun Corps. Operation Order No. 47. Appendix III	14/08/1918	14/08/1918
Operation(al) Order(s)	27th Battalion Machine Gun Corps. Operation Order No. 47. Appendix IV	11/08/1918	11/08/1918
Operation(al) Order(s)	Amendment to 37th Battn. M.G. Corps Operation Order No. 47	15/08/1918	15/08/1918
Operation(al) Order(s)	27th Battalion, Machine Gun Corps. Operation Order No. 48. Appendix V	19/08/1918	19/08/1918

Operation(al) Order(s)	Instructions Nos. 1 and 2. (Supplementary to 37th Bn. M.G.C. Order No. 48.)	20/08/1918	20/08/1918
Miscellaneous	M.G. 257. Appendix VI	22/08/1918	22/08/1918
Heading	37th Bn Machine Gun Corps. War Diary for the month of September 1918 Vol 7		
War Diary		01/09/1918	09/09/1918
War Diary	Favreuil	10/09/1918	10/09/1918
War Diary	Velu Wood	11/09/1918	20/09/1918
War Diary	Le Barque	21/09/1918	29/09/1918
War Diary	Bertincourt	30/09/1918	30/09/1918
Operation(al) Order(s)	37th Battalion Machine Gun Corps. Operation Order No. 49. Appendix I	13/09/1918	13/09/1918
Operation(al) Order(s)	37th Battalion Machine Gun Corps. Order No. 12 Appendix II	20/09/1918	20/09/1918
Heading	37th Bn Machine Gun Corps. War Diary for the month of October 1918 Vol 8		
War Diary		01/10/1918	31/10/1918
Heading	37th Bn Machine Gun Corps War Diary for month of November 1918 Vol 10		
War Diary		01/11/1918	30/11/1918
Heading	37th Bn. M.G.C. War Diary for the month of December 1918. Vol 10		
War Diary		01/12/1918	31/12/1918
Heading	War Diary 37 Bn Machine Gun Corps Month of January 1919 Vol 12		
War Diary	Gosselies.	01/01/1919	28/02/1919
War Diary	Gosselies Belgium	01/03/1919	31/03/1919
War Diary	Mulheim.	01/05/1919	31/05/1919

WO 95/2524/2

37 Bn Machine Gun Corps

March 1916 - March 1919

BEF

37 Div Troops

37 Bn M.G. Corps

1918 MAR - 1919 MAR

37 Bn M.G. Corps

Army Form C. 2118.

WAR DIARY
or
INTELLIGENCE SUMMARY.
(Erase heading not required.)

Instructions regarding War Diaries and Intelligence Summaries are contained in F. S. Regs., Part II. and the Staff Manual respectively. Title pages will be prepared in manuscript.

Place	Date	Hour	Summary of Events and Information	Remarks and references to Appendices
BRISTOL CAMP	4.3.18		The 37th Battalion M.G.C. was formed from the 4 Machine Gun Companies the 63rd, the 111th, 112th, and 247th Coys. Lieut-Col. W.W. Prescott-Westcar, D.S.O. took over command, Major E.M.G. Medical D.S.O assumed duties of 2/ic. Capt. R.H. Rogers, Adjutant, H/Lt Purves Transport Officer. Coys were called A,B,C&D respectively. B,A&D Coys were holding the Divisional Front (MENIN ROAD Sector YPRES) & 'C' Coy were at BRISTOK CAMP. A counter preparation took place, all guns firing on SOS lines.	
DICKEBUSCH AREA				
BRISTOL CAMP (BHQ) & LINE	5-3-18 to 10-3-18		During this period A,B&D Companies remained in the line, A&D Coys carrying out relief by small parties. Although the trenches were heavily shelled on several occasions, no casualties occurred. Lieut. F.J. Beckman joined the 15th in 6-3-18 and took over command of "C" Coy from Lieut. G. Palmer. Usual routine was carried out in the trenches & training by the Company at rest in Camp.	
- do -	11.3.18		2/Lt Anderson joined the 13th 8-3-18 & took over command of A Coy. Special report for 9th attached. 2/Lt Storey Rgy & 1.0.R presumed killed. "C" Coy relieved B Coy in the line. B Coy returned to Bristol Camp. "B" Coy on the right of the West Road. B Coy being 'A' on the right, 'C' Coy centre & D Coy on the left. & C.A.A dumps improved at the various Coy H.Q. "D" Coy carried out counter preparation according to arranged programme.	
- do -	12.3.18 to 14.3.18		Usual trench routine carried out, also training at Bristol Camp. Casualties in the line O.R.1	
- do -	15.3.18		C & D Coy co-operated with 112th Bgde. who carried out a raid on enemy trenches left of the MENIN ROAD. Casualties nil.	
	16.3.18 to 18.3.18		A, C & D Coys still in the line. Hostile enemy trench mortar. A number of reinforcements joined the Bn. more than had. Casualties 2 O.R wounded.	
	19.3.18		C & A Companies co-operated in a raid made by the Somerset's. Guns S/C of 2 Lieut Thompson delivered enemy Machine Guns and other guns carried out effective fire. The raid was a success & congratulations were received from the Corps Commander. C Coy were relieved by B Coy.	

Army Form C. 2118.

WAR DIARY
or
INTELLIGENCE SUMMARY.
(Erase heading not required.)

Instructions regarding War Diaries and Intelligence Summaries are contained in F. S. Regs., Part II. and the Staff Manual respectively. Title pages will be prepared in manuscript.

Place	Date	Hour	Summary of Events and Information	Remarks and references to Appendices
LINE & BRISTOL CAMP, Nr Dickelbusch, Belgium	20.3.18 to 24.3.18		Nothing unusual to report. Work & and patrols was carried out by companies in the line. The Companies in camp were employed in improving the condition of the camp. Casualties 3 O.R. wounded.	
	25.3.18		B Coy were relieved by A & D Coys. B Coy returned to Bristol Camp. A & D Coys continued to hold the line.	
	26.3.18		Lieut. Cunliffe was killed by a shell as he was leaving to his Divisional Front. M.G. 13 in SHREWSBURY FOREST SECTOR	
	27.3.18		C Coy relieved the 1st Coy Australian M.G.C.	
Lemins	27.3.18		A & C Coy were relieved by the H.Q. 13th M.G.C. & returned to BRISTOL CAMP and later proceeded to billets in BOESCHEPE. B Coy proceeded by motor busses to CASTRE A Coy and B Coy H.Q. proceeded to CABLE CAMP near RENNINGHELST, D Coy to POPLAR CAMP Companies rested throughout the day.	
	28.3.18	10 a.m 9.15 a.m	A Coy entrained at HOPOUTRE and detrained at BOQUEMAISON B Coy entrained at CASTRE and detrained at MONTICOURT and proceeded by road to TOUTENCOURT C Coy — — — — — — to GRENAS	
	29.3.18	10 a.m	D Coy & Bn H.Q. entrained at HOPOUTRE & detrained at BOQUEMAISON.	
	29.3.18		A Coy marched to DOULLENS, thence by train to AMIENS and thence by road to PONT NOYELLE	
	30.3.18		A Coy marched to MARIEUX, B Coy to AUTHIE, C Coy rested in billets at GRENAS & D Coy together with Bn HQ moved to POMMERA	
	31.3.18		D Coy & Bn. H.Q. remained at POMMERA, A Coy at MARIEUX & B Coy at AUTHIE.	

Capt.
Alphabd 37th 13th Machine Gun Corps

Special Report on Operations (M/G)
on Left Sector, by Lt. W.P. Weares. 206"D"Coy. MG HQ
In the Field.   9th March 1918.

1. On the night of 8th March, 28 O.R. reported to Coy HQ to strengthen the 12 teams already in the line, & to man the 4 reserve guns in GLENCORSE WOOD TUNNELS.
Two of the 12 defence guns became permanently out of action on the night of the 8th, through mechanical breakdown, & were replaced by 2 of the reserve guns, reducing the guns in reserve to 2. (Vide M/G Rtn)
One of the reserve guns was kept in the Champagne Emplacement Tunnels (J.14.b.35.29), & the other was moved before dawn (9th) & placed at about J.9.d.9.9 at my responsibility, — to give greater strength to left flank, by direct fire.
On the morning of the 9th I visited the G.O.C. 111th Inf. Bde. at RAILWAY HOUSE. He discussed the situation with me; stated that he regretted having so little M/G. S.O.S. support on his sector, — & that he considered the area J.16.b required more attention. He enquired about the reserve guns, & I explained the situation. He approved of one gun being kept in reserve at about J.9.d.9.9, & instructed me to inform the C.O, M/G. Bn. of this.

2. The enemy artillery kept up a barrage all day (commencing about 9 a.m.) on our front line & supports — confined almost entirely to within 1000 x of our front line.

3. The S.O.S. went up on our left at 5.45 p.m., — & a smoke barrage was put up by the enemy across our front. Our S.O.S. guns opened fire immediately on their lines, in conjunction with the artillery. Soon afterwards, the S.O.S. was sent up on our right, — & then across front. The rate of fire of our M/G. followed that of the artillery, which ceased fire about 8 p.m.

4. I kept in touch with the O.C. 13th R.R.R. & 10th R.F. (- both in GLENCORSE TUNNELS, the latter having moved forward in support).

At 7.30 pm I was informed that the JOPPA trench system was in the hands of the enemy, — the situation in the JHERICO system being uncertain. I at once directed a barrage behind this area, on J.1.b.a. & J.2.y.b., having first obtained the actual dispositions of our forward posts from the O.C. Ins. (ref "clearance.")

Later I heard that the enemy had made his original approach via the REUTELBEEK, — & placed 2 guns across the valley in J.1.b.d. Eventually, acting on the advice of the O.C. 10th R.F. (who was in charge of the counter-attack operations) — I placed the whole of the guns of D11 & D12 Batteries (8 guns) along the line J.22.b.3.5, 1.b.d.5.0, 1.b.d.5.5, 1.b.d.3.7, 1.b.d.3.9. Fire was maintained on these lines until daybreak – every available man belt-filling.

Total rounds fired between 5.40 pm. 8th & daybreak 9th, — 81,000.

5. It was reported at 7.30 am. this morning (9th) that all the ground captured by the enemy last night had been retaken.

6. Casualties up to 6 am. 9th. 1 O.R. wounded

7. All guns working well at 6 am 9th.

8. <u>Signal Communications.</u> These were good between O.H.Q, D.12 & D.13 until 7.30 pm. when Fullerphone at O.H.Q. became out of order (wires cut) The arrangement whereby O.H.Q. was to communicate with D.11 — by buried cable, proved useless, as the line was always engaged. I will endeavour to obtain authority to lay a separate wire from O.H.Q. to D.11.

H.G. Stearns. Lt.

IV.Corps.

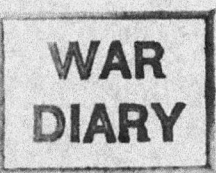

37th BATTALION, MACHINE GUN CORPS.

A P R I L

1 9 1 8

Attached:

Operation Orders.
Tracings.

Army Form C. 2118.

37 Bn M.G. Corps

Secret

WAR DIARY and INTELLIGENCE SUMMARY.

(Erase heading not required.)

Instructions regarding War Diaries and Intelligence Summaries are contained in F.S. Regs., Part II. and the Staff Manual respectively. Title pages will be prepared in manuscript.

Map Sheet 57d NE

Place	Date	Hour	Summary of Events and Information	Remarks and references to Appendices
MARIEUX AUTHIE GRENAS	1.4.18	9 a.m.	"A" Coy. left MARIEUX and after a short march bivouaced between BIENVILLERS and SOUASTRE. Later in the day the Coy. moved up to the line and relieved one Coy. of the 62nd Bn. M.G.C. in the HEB_nterne Sector. Casualties NIL. B.Coy. 2/Lt AUTHIE at proceeded to HENUE where they billeted for the night. C.Coy. under Lt. 2/c moved from GRENAS to COURN. O.C. Coy. reconnoitred the line D.Coy. Proceeded by road to PAS and billeted for the night. Transport Lines at BAYENCOURT. B.H.Q. at SOUASTRE. Weather very wet and cold.	
HEBUTERNE DIV. SECTOR	2.4.18		A Coy. in the line with Coy HQ at PIGEON WOOD. Improvement on our positions carried out. B.Coy. Prepared for the line and at night relieved one Coy. of the 62nd Bn. M.G.C. Relief was completed about 11pm. Casualties nil. C.Coy. relieved one Coy. of 62nd Bn. M.G.C. in the BIEZ WOOD SECTOR, with Coy HQ at RETTMOY FARM. Relief was completed about 11.15 pm. Casualties NIL. Guns were disposed as follows:- 4 guns in the SUNKEN ROAD between BIEZ WOOD and ROSSIGNOL WOOD. 4 guns in E30.C. 2 guns E9a.69. D.Coy. relieved one Coy. of the 62nd Bn. M.G.C., relief being complete about 11.45 pm. Casualties nil. Weather continues wet and unsettled.	
— do —	3.4.18		Situation in the line remained quiet throughout the day but enemy movement was active, also enemy aircraft. Work on gun positions & trenches was carried out but owing to the wet weather and bad condition of the trenches, work was difficult and the men suffered severely from the mud & wet. Harassing fire on selected targets in enemy lines was carried out during the night. 1 O.R. were wounded.	
— do —	4.4.18		Enemy artillery were active. Companies carried out counter preparation in view of an attack on ROSSIGNOL WOOD. 2/Lieut. Robinson was wounded by rifle bullet and Capt & Adjutant R.B. Rogers was had proceeded to the line was also wounded. 2 O.R. wounded. Harassing fire on cross roads and tracks was continued throughout the night. Weather continues unsettled & visibility is poor.	
— do —	5.4.18	5.30	The Infantry moved forward in attack on ROSSIGNOL WOOD. M.G. Coys. supporting as follows:- A Coy. from ZERO HOUR, 5.30 am. to ZERO plus 75, 10,000 rds. S.A.A. were fired on K.15.E.50.60 and 17.E. 70.30. Enemy retaliated with heavy shelling & gas. Casualties 8. O.R. wounded. B.Coy. Carried out harassing fire. C.Coy. In conjunction with the Somerset Light Infantry of the 63rd Brigade. One section under 2/Lt. J. Woollin advanced under cover of our artillery & MG barrage and obtained a direct fire into ROSSIGNOL WOOD of 200 yards range. Following a sudden lift the WOOD had been taken, he pushed forward but a heavy fire was opened on him from the WOOD & two of the number one were killed. N was quite exhausted	

Army Form C. 2118.

WAR DIARY
or
INTELLIGENCE SUMMARY.
(Erase heading not required.)

Instructions regarding War Diaries and Intelligence Summaries are contained in F. S. Regs., Part II. and the Staff Manual respectively. Title pages will be prepared in manuscript.

Remarks and references to Appendices: Map Sheet 57d NE

Place	Date	Hour	Summary of Events and Information
HEBUTERNE Sector			that the enemy still held the WOOD. A cheer was heard. The enemy attacked in considerable force the village of BUCQUOI and the Infy were seen to be retiring. Under cover of a heavy bombardment the enemy succeeded in entering the village. Two guns were disabled and in conformity with Bde orders
		5.4.18	our guns were withdrawn. During the attack by our troops, guns of No.4 Section also 1 section of D Coy carried out overhead fire, also swept the approaches to LA LOUVIERE FARM & PUISIEUX. About 5000 rds were fired. Casualties 5 killed and 4 wounded.
			During the attack, the enemy fired a heavy barrage on roads & wagon on the back areas. The Transport at BAYENCOURT suffered heavily, 4 O.R. being killed and 17 wounded, 30 animals were also killed and wounded. Transport lines moved to SURCAMPS near SOUASTRE.
			Total casualties for the day 9 killed, 27 wounded. The weather was fair and visibility bad.
	6.4.18		In morning & general fire & the situation was fairly quiet. During the afternoon information was received that the enemy were massing in a sunken road at K.7.c & D and guns of A Coy immediately opened a heavy fire, firing about 10000 rds.
			B Coy carried out sides Coy relief.
			C Coy. No.4 Section relieved 2 guns of A Coy & 2 guns of B Coy west of BUCQUOI in the reserve line at L.2.6. Similar preparation was carried out. By Morley joined the Coy in the field and was posted to No.4 Section.
			Total casualties 1 O.R. 4.30.R wounded.
	7.4.18		Re-organization of guns was carried out during the night 6/7th and were disposed as under.
			A Coy withdrew to the Transport lines
			B Coy. 2 guns at approx T.1.C.4.5. 2 guns at approx K.6.d.4.2. 4 guns in Battery at E.30.d.6.6. 4 guns in K.5.d. C.C. and 11.E.
			4 guns in approx K.6. to sweep with direct fire S.E. direction.
			C Coy. 6 guns K.25.d. L.1A. and d.
			4 guns in T.2. to cover BUCQUOI
			2 guns in T.1.d.
			4 guns in E.30.c.
			D Coy. 12 guns in PURPLE LINE. 2 guns at approx. K.10.d. 2 guns 18.10.a.

Army Form C. 2118.

WAR DIARY or INTELLIGENCE SUMMARY.
(Erase heading not required.)

Remarks and references to Appendices: Map Sheet 57D NE

Place	Date	Hour	Summary of Events and Information
	7-4-18 continued		There was intermittent shelling on both sides throughout the day. Enemy aircraft was very active. Slight fire on selected targets was carried out as usual. Casualties 2 O.R. wounded.
	8-4-18		Weather conditions were slightly better and visibility improved. The situation throughout the day was quiet. Re-organization of gun positions took place and were disposed as under. B.Coy. 4 guns in F.30.c.50.35. 4 guns in vicinity K.6.a.40.55. 4 guns in E.29.c. 4 guns at K.5.q. C.Coy. 4 guns in vicinity F.25.c.40.00. 2 guns L.1.d.50.80. 4 guns in reserve in dug-outs vicinity F.25.c.10.60. 4 guns return to Transport lines. D.Coy. withdraw 8 guns from E.29.c & K.5.a to dug-outs in F.25.c. A.Coy. carried out training at the Transport lines.
	9-4-18		Enemy artillery was active throughout the day but no casualties occurred. Visual harrassing fire was carried on during the night. B.Coy. 4 guns were moved from COD ST. to K.5.a.77. 4 guns from F.30.d.6.6 to F.30.c.4.2. 2 guns from K.6.a.5.1 & 2 from INC.4.3 to F.29. The 8 guns of D Coy. in F.28.B. took over positions K.14.6. K.9.6 & K.3.C.
	10-4-18		There was little activity on the front. The weather continues to be unsettled & visibility was poor. Visual trench routine carried out. Casualties Nil.
	11-4-18		Artillery on both sides were active, especially in Corkarra's "C" Coy relieved Hostile M.G. in FORK WOOD, 3000 rds being fired.
	12-4-18		B Coy dispersed enemy working party. C Coy engaged LA LOUVIERE FM & enemy trenches in t.14.a. from RATTEMOY FARM. Hostile artillery shelled position. Reinf'ts about 7pm. 2/Lt. Gregson was wounded, also 2 O.R.
	13-4-18		The situation throughout the day was quiet. 4 guns of the 62nd Division relieved 4 guns of D Coy & other positions were altered and guns disposed as follows.

Army Form C. 2118.

WAR DIARY
or
INTELLIGENCE SUMMARY.
(Erase heading not required.)

Instructions regarding War Diaries and Intelligence Summaries are contained in F. S. Regs., Part II. and the Staff Manual respectively. Title pages will be prepared in manuscript.

Map Sheet 57D NE

Place	Date	Hour	Summary of Events and Information	Remarks and references to Appendices
Hebuterne Sector	13.4.18		**A.Coy.** H.Q. in HEBUTERNE CAVES at R.d 30.70. 2 guns in K.10.d. 4 guns K.10.6. 2 guns K.9.6. 2 guns in K.3.C. 4 guns in K.14.a.	
			B.Coy. H.Q. in E.28. 4 guns in E.29, E.30, K.5 and K.6. also 2 guns of C.Coy under O.C. B.Coy in L.1.C.	
			C.Coy. 4 guns in K.1.a. 2 guns K.7.C. 8 guns at Transport Lines.	
			D.Coy. 5 guns at Transport Lines. 4 guns in reserve in E.28. 2 guns in K.5.C. 2 guns in K.4.a, 2 in K.10.a and 1 in K.4.c.	
	14.4.18		**A.Coy.** 1 gun team proceeded to the line and took up a position at K.16.a.33¼.	
			B.Coy. Enemy observed behind ROSSIGNOL WOOD in full marching order. Fire was immediately opened and searched the area for two hours.	
			C.Coy. Teams at Transport Lines carried out training	
			D.Coy. Report that their water was faulty, settled during the day. All guns detailed for harrassing fire, carried out programme as arranged & swept tracks and roads in rear of the enemy lines. Casualties for the day 3 O.R. wounded.	
	15.4.18		Enemy artillery was very active throughout the day. The weather was dull and cold and observation was very poor. B.Coy. engaged an enemy working party but the result of the fire could not be observed. Our guns fired at intervals throughout the night. Casualties 3. O.R. wounded.	
	16.4.18		Enemy artillery was again very active and shelled the sector intermittently throughout the day but no casualties occurred. Visibility was again very poor.	
	17.4.18 17.4.18		On the night 17/18th the Bn. were relieved by the 14th Bn M.G.C. H.Q, A, B & D Coys. proceeding to huts in AUTHIE WOOD and C Coy to camp was down. Relief was completed by about 1 a.m. on the 18th. Casualties Nil.	

D. D. & L. London, B.C.
(A801) Wt. W1771/M2031 750,000 5/17 Sch. 52 Forms/C2118/14

Army Form C. 2118.

MAP SHEET
57 D NE

WAR DIARY
or
INTELLIGENCE SUMMARY.
(Erase heading not required.)

Instructions regarding War Diaries and Intelligence Summaries are contained in F. S. Regs., Part II. and the Staff Manual respectively. Title pages will be prepared in manuscript.

Place	Date	Hour	Summary of Events and Information	Remarks and references to Appendices
ANTHIE WOOD	18.4.18		Accommodation in the Camp was very poor and about noon a move was made to the BOIS DU WARNIMONT. The Bn were now in Corps Reserve and were under orders to move at short notice in case of enemy Penetration of the line in the neighbourhood of COIGNEUX P.S.	
BOIS du WARNIMONT	19.4.18		The day was spent in cleaning and inspecting arms and kit, etc. The weather was very bad & snow showers were frequent throughout the day.	
"	20.4.18		Companies engaged in training. BCoy occupied the reserve line (RED LINE) for practice. C Coy carried out a tactical scheme in the morning and in the afternoon, a practice alarm for occupation of the RED LINE was given. D Coy carried out training during the morning & in the afternoon it to proceed to the Bois des Alleux. Wine	
"	21.4.18		The day was spent quietly. All small Box respirators were inspected by the Bde Gas Officer.	
"	22.4.18		Service was held during the afternoon. The weather was slightly better.	
"	23.4.18		The four companies continued training. Several tactical schemes were carried out.	
"	24.4.18		On the night 34/25th 2 Coys relieved 2 Coys of the 62nd Bn BlWG Coy on the BCoy relieved D Coy of the 62nd Bn & C Coy relieved B Coy. Guns were disposed as follows BCoy under Capt. Smaller in the old British front line in front of FONQUEVILLERS. 2 guns in E.28.a.05.20. firing South. 2 guns in E.22.d.15.00 firing East. 2 guns in E.28.a.60.45. firing S.E. 2 guns in E.22.b.05.95. firing East. 2 guns in E.22.c.50.55 firing East. 2 guns in E.22.b.25.15 firing S.E. under orders of Capt. Smaller. C Coy 2 guns in I.1.d.30.55. firing Southwards into I.7.a. 2 guns in I.1.a.25.05. firing S. into I.2.c. 2 guns in F.25.d.68.20 flanking the edge of BIEZ WOOD. 2 guns in F.25.d.10.90 for dug towards L.2. central. 4 guns in F.36.d.80.40 flanking the Southern blocks of HAMEL HILL. 2 guns in F.26.b.45.95 for dug forward BUCQUOY and 2 guns in F.27.a.60.90 also firing towards BUCQUOY. Relief was completed about 10.30 p.m. Casualties Nil. Weather unsettled Under orders of GHQRE. Major Beadman acting under orders of S.O.C. RIGHT BGDE	

Army Form C. 2118.

WAR DIARY
or
INTELLIGENCE SUMMARY.
(Erase heading not required.)

Instructions regarding War Diaries and Intelligence Summaries are contained in F. S. Regs., Part II. and the Staff Manual respectively. Title pages will be prepared in manuscript.

MAP Sheet 57D. NE

Place	Date	Hour	Summary of Events and Information	Remarks and references to Appendices
BUCQUOY SECTOR	25.4.18		"B"&"C" Coys in the line. Schaeken guard. The weather was bright and fine but visibility was only fair on the night 23/24th. A Coy relieved "C" Coy and B.13th M.G.C. and D Coy relieved A Coy 62nd M.G.C. Relief was completed by about midnight — Casualties Nil. Guns disposed as follows:—	
			"A" Coy. 4 guns in F.21.c.25.40 firing S.E. 2 guns in F.21.d.30.80 firing S.E. 2 guns in F.18.b.90.80 firing towards Fdg central. 2 guns in F.22.b.05.95 firing East. 4 guns in F.15.c.10.10 firing East and S.E. 2 guns in F.14.d.75.20 firing East and Bank East. 2 guns in F.14.d.50.10 firing East & S.E. Under command of Major Caddy + acting under orders of G.O.C. LEFT BGDE	
			D Coy. 2 guns in F.30.a.20.20 firing S.E. 2 guns in F.36.a.90.45 firing S.E. 2 guns in E.24.d.80.15 firing S.E. 2 guns in E.24.d.38.90 — " — S.E. 4 guns in F.13.c.25.10 firing East and S.E. 2 guns in F.13.c.70.00 firing East and S.E. 2 guns in F.19.b.75.05 firing East + S.E. Under Command of Major Tylor + acting under orders of G.O.C. reserve Bgde. Bn. H.Q. at HENU.	
	26.4.18		Artillery was active on both sides. With assistance of the R.E.'s, improvement of gun positions was carried out. There was a good deal of rain throughout the day and visibility was poor. Harassing fire was carried out during the night. Casualties Nil.	
	27.4.18		Visibility was again poor but the weather throughout the day was fine and warm. Enemy artillery was very active throughout the day. A Coy. Guns not firing. B Coy. Still in Divisional reserve. Matthey Inspected. C Coy. Hostile M.G.s active during the night + harassed position F.26 d + BIEZ WOOD. D Coy. New emplacement constructed at E.30.a.30.05 rous team from F.30 & 10.45 moved there. Enemy M.G. firing from about ROSSIGNOL WOOD harassed our positions in E.24.C. + F.30.C. constructed at E.24.d.20.00. during the night. Casualties Nil—	1600 the fired on target 10.A.45.65 2000 " " " " " 28.d.10.80 2500 " — " — 2.A.c.9.9 Many alternative positions 1600 the fired on target F.26 d. + BIEZ WOOD.

Army Form C. 2118.

WAR DIARY
or
INTELLIGENCE SUMMARY.

(Erase heading not required.)

Place	Date	Hour	Summary of Events and Information	Remarks and references to Appendices
BUCQUOY SECTOR	28/7/18		Visibility was good throughout the day, especially towards evening. Artillery was extremely active on both sides and increased towards night.	M+P. Sheet 57d.NE
			A.Coy. Gun not firing. Work on emplacement & dugouts continued & emplacement for Anti-Aircraft gun was completed. Two guns moved from F.28.b. to approximately L.1.d.	
			B.Coy. In reserve in FONQUEVILLERS. Nothing to report	
			C.Coy. report hostile Machine guns active throughout the night, sweeping our gun position at F.27.a. & our gun firing in short bursts of harassing fire on to the village of Bucquoy and gassed area F.26.c. Gun firing from direction of Bucquoy swept parapet of trenches in L.2.d. Our guns carried out night fire. 15,000 rds being fired on targets L.8.d.5.5., L.4.c.9.7. & road in L.13.a.	
			D.Coy. Hostile guns from direction of ROSSIGNOL WOOD harassed ESSARTS - GOMMECOURT ROAD throughout the night. Our guns not firing. Casualties. Total. 1.O.R. wounded by shell fire.	
-do-	29/7/18		Situation Normal. Weather dull and cloudy with occasional showers. Artillery on both sides was very active. Between 9-11a.m. enemy dropped about 60. 5.9" in vicinity of BETTEMOY FARM and PIGEON WOOD. BIEZ WOOD, L.10.35-65, F.26 & F.37 was shelled intermittently throughout the day.	
			A.Coy. } Gun not firing. Enemy guns from near The CRUCIFIX in BUCQUOY firing throughout the night at intervals B.Coy. }	
			C.Coy. Enemy M.G.'s swept our positions in F.35.d. throughout the night. M.G. bullets from SW direction striking around positions L.2.b. 65.15. Enemy guns firing from direction of BUCQUOY & L.1.d. firing over position L.2.d. 40.90. & sweeping Southern Edge of BIEZ WOOD & positions at L.1.d. 35-65. Our guns in position F.26.A.9.4. fired on targets & tracks in L.10.a. & b., L.4.c. central b.& F.5.A.00, L.4.C. - do - { F.15-d.65-30} fired on tracks in L.4.C. and L.& D { F.15-d.80-50} Total RAA expended 15,000 rds.	
			D.Coy. Nothing to report. Work on new emplacements & dug outs continued in conjunction with the R.E's. Parties employed. 2 Hostile aircraft crossed our lines but were driven back again by Anti-aircraft defences. Casualties 1.O.R. wounded	

Army Form C. 2118.

WAR DIARY
or
INTELLIGENCE SUMMARY.

(Erase heading not required.)

Place	Date	Hour	Summary of Events and Information	Remarks and references to Appendices
	30/4/18		Weather throughout the day was dull and showery, visibility very poor. Artillery on both sides was very active QUESNOY FARM~ BUCQUOY was shelled at odd intervals, also BIEZ WOOD, PIGEON WOOD and the PURPLE LINE in E.30.a.	
			A Coy. Work on emplacements continued. Baby elephant shelters are being erected at Gun positions in F.15.C. Harassing fire on targets F.29.C.75.35 to F.29.C.90.45 & F.24.a.40.48, 5000 rds being fired. Enemy guns were also active during the night.	
			B Coy. Nothing to report.	
			C Coy. The usual night harassing fires in conjunction with the Artillery Barrage were carried on on tracks and occupied territory in rear of enemy lines. Hostile guns were again active throughout the night firing from directions of BUCQUOY and ROSSIGNAL WOOD. Weather prohibited any aircraft activity.	
			D Coy. Enemy M Guns were active during the night about F.24.d.50.55 from BUCQUOY direction. Tracks in E.30.a+b. went also subjected to night harassing fire. New emplacement was made at E.24.d.45.55 and camouflaged Gun from F.24.C.90.30 was moved to this new emplacement. Work on new emplacements at F.19.a +F.19.a +L.53 was continued. Work on dug-outs and trenches was also carried out.	
			Casualties, O.R. 3. wounded.	

Bron Whatr Lieut-Colonel
Comdg 37th Bn Machine Gun Corps.
1-5-1918.

OPERATION ORDERS.

Army Form C. 2118.

37 Bn M.G. Corps

MAY 1918

WAR DIARY
or
INTELLIGENCE SUMMARY.

(Erase heading not required.)

Instructions regarding War Diaries and Intelligence Summaries are contained in F.S. Regs., Part II. and the Staff Manual respectively. Title pages will be prepared in manuscript.

Place	Date	Hour	Summary of Events and Information	Remarks and references to Appendices
			Refce: MAP. Sheet 57.D. NE 1/20000	
BUCQUOY Sector	1-5-18		Our Artillery was very active throughout the day. Enemy artillery was also very active, shelling areas F.26.b and F.27.a. F.25.b. PIGEON WOOD, ROTTENROY FARM, GOMMECOURT-ESSARTS-ROAD and SQUARE WOOD. The weather was cold and dull. Visibility poor owing to low clouds and mist. A. Coy. Not firing. During the night hostile M.G. fired on the track near No.1. Redan (F.21.B.75.35). Work on trenches was carried out and shelters made for ammunition. 2/Lieut. R.A. Faulkner proceeded to the Transport Lines sick. B. Coy. in reserve on old British Front Line in front of FONQUEVILLERS. Situation normal. C. Coy. Gun positions filled with T. Bars. In F.13.d.H.4 work commenced on new emplacement. Work on trenches carried out. Hostile MG's were active during the night from direction of FORK WOOD against F.26.a. Another gun firing from about F.29 and F.21.e. swept parapet at I.2.d.40.90. Another M.G. swept the ridge in F.21 & 22. Gun firing from direction of BUCQUOY. Our guns were active throughout the night on tracks and light railways in rear of enemy lines at approximate I.4.C.65. F.25.C.32. Bright railway in F.10.a. and tracks in F.4.C. Total rounds fired 9,750. D. Coy. Work on day only made. M.Gs was contined at F.13.C.36, also work on new emplacement at F.19.a. central, near F.19.a.42.53 and F.19.d.20.55. Shelters for S.A.A., tell boxes and stores were made. Enemy M.G. firing from direction of F.8.d. harrased GOMMECOURT-ESSARTS-ROAD, F.14.d. and F.30.B. throughout the night. Our guns not firing. Aircraft activity Nil. Casualties: 1 man wounded by shell fire. B.H.Q. and Transport lines at HENU. Advanced B.H.Q. at FONQUEVILLERS. Reserve gunners at the Transport Lines carried out training.	
BUCQUOY SECTOR	2-5-18		The weather was bright and fine throughout the day and visibility was good. Aircraft was active throughout the day on both sides. 36 enemy aircraft flew over our lines in F.30.a.b. at 8.20am but were driven back by our M.G. fire. Hostile 3.05pm enemy planes attempted to fly the 9.1 Schul our lines but was driven back by A.A. fire. Our aircraft were up continually throughout the day, picking up lines will add	

Army Form C. 2118.

WAR DIARY
or
INTELLIGENCE SUMMARY.

(Erase heading not required.)

Instructions regarding War Diaries and Intelligence Summaries are contained in F. S. Regs., Part II. and the Staff Manual respectively. Title pages will be prepared in manuscript.

Place	Date	Hour	Summary of Events and Information	Remarks and references to Appendices
Bucquoy Sector	2/5/18		The enemy lines. At night our planes bombed enemy rear areas most noticeably in direction of ACHIET-LE-VILLE. There was considerable increase in hostile artillery particularly in areas E.24.d. 05.90 to F.21.c. 60.20, about 300 5.9's being dropped. About 500 4.2 x 5.9s were dropped in areas F.26.b & F.27.a. ASSARTS, QUESNOY FARM, areas F.21.d., 25.d. F.13.a. Rka., I.1.b, & 14.c. and 30.c. were shelled intermittently throughout the day. A.Coy. Work on trenches, dug outs, + new emplacements was continued. B.Coy. Nothing to report. C.Coy. 2 Guns sited in F.26.a.9. engaged enemy aircraft between noon and 6p.m. 5000 rounds being fired. " " F.26.b. 60.90 " " " " " " " 600 " Our guns carried out harassing fire throughout the night on tracks and occupied areas in I.14.c. 32, 55, I.A.c.80.95, I.M.c. I.10.a. 45.55. 7000 rounds being fired. Mobile guns sited in our trenches in F.26.A + B from direction of YORK WOOD. Work on trenches and positions was continued. Anti-aircraft position at F.15.d. 80.50 being constructed. F.26.6 A.A. position completed + trench deepened, I.1.d. #6 trench deepened. D.Coy. Enemy guns harassed tracks in F.30.a. x c. throughout the night. Gun firing from direction of ROSSIGNOL WOOD. Enemy guns not firing. Work on dug outs at F-13.c. C.35.00 was continued under direction of R.E's. Trench at F.19.C.8.3 revetted. Emplacement at F.34. d. 50.50 continued + nearing completion. Total casualties 12 other ranks gassed.	
BUCQUOY SECTOR	3.5.18		After an early morning mist visibility was good throughout the day. There was considerable aircraft activity on both sides. Several enemy machines crossed our lines at intervals, one flying low fired M.G. at the front line. Our machines repeatedly crossed the enemy lines in spite of heavy A.A. fire. Enemy Artillery continued to be very active, particularly shelling areas F.26.b + F.26.a., E.3.a, I.1.c., I.1.a + B and F.30.c. H.762 WOOD was heavily bombarded with shrapnel about 11p.m. Our Artillery was also active, and ROSSIGNOL WOOD was heavily bombarded. Harassing fire on tracks, roads and occupied areas were carried out during the night.	80.2

Army Form C. 2118.

MAY WAR DIARY and INTELLIGENCE SUMMARY.

(Erase heading not required.)

Instructions regarding War Diaries and Intelligence Summaries are contained in F. S. Regs, Part II. and the Staff Manual respectively. Title pages will be prepared in manuscript.

Place	Date	Hour	Summary of Events and Information	Remarks and references to Appendices
BUCQUOY SECTOR	3/5/18		**A.Coy:** Our guns engaged enemy aircraft on several occasions during the day – no visible effect. No night firing to report. Work on improving tracks and dug-outs continued. Shelters completed, all each gun position to take 6 belt boxes. Baby elephant shelters for gun teams are nearing completion.	
			B.Coy. 2 guns were moved from F.22.d.18 to new positions in F.21.c.30 and 2 guns from F.21.B. to new positions in F.22.B. Guns not firing.	
			C.Coy. Our guns fired on targets as follows. 9pm to 6pm at intervals 2000 rds at enemy planes. 6.30pm to 10.30pm 3000 rds on tracks & road in I.10.a. 9pm to 11pm 2000 rds on main road in I.4.d. 3am to 5am. Guns at F.25.d.45.90 and F.25d.80.50 fired about 2000 rds on targets I.4.c.32.85 & I.4.c.50.15. Guns at F.26.B.60.90 fired about 2000 rds on road I.4.central. Hostile guns were active throughout the night, especially from direction of YORK WOOD against our trenches on the ridge in F.26.a. Work on Trenches. I.1.d.4.6. French deepened & dug out entrance filled with elephant shelter. F.25.d.45.90 work under R.B's on dug-out continued. F.27.a.55.85. Shaft completed & tunnel lengthened 5 feet.	
			D.Coy. Guns not firing. Work on dug-outs indicated at F.13.c.3500 was continued under R.E's. Work on new emplacements at F.19.a.central and F.19.a.45.55 continued. Alternative emplacement at F.20.a.00.55 commenced. Steel emplacement at F.14.d.50.50 completed and camouflaged. Dug-out and trench at F.20.a.30.00 improved.	
			Casualties for the 24 hours, NIL.	
			A number of enemy observation balloons were up at intervals throughout the day at – grid bearings of 72°, 92°, 100°, 145° from F.26.a.8.4.	
			Enemy aeroplane dropped a red paper balloon at about F.14.D. containing German Newspapers and notices to French Civilians. These were taken by the Guards B'de.	

MAY 1918
WAR DIARY or INTELLIGENCE SUMMARY.

Army Form C. 2118.

Instructions regarding War Diaries and Intelligence Summaries are contained in F. S. Regs., Part II. and the Staff Manual respectively. Title pages will be prepared in manuscript.

(Erase heading not required.)

Place	Date	Hour	Summary of Events and Information	Remarks and references to Appendices
BUCQUOY SECTOR	4-5-18		During the day there was normal Artillery Activity on both sides. The enemy shelled the following areas. E.24. F.31.b, F.22.c. F.25.b. F.27.a, L.10. L.2.d at various times during the day. He bombed ROSSIGNOL WOOD in E.12 heavily during the day. Enemy Machine Gun Harassed E.30.a.6 F.27.a and F.20.b during the night 3/4 th May. Visibility was fairly high during the day. A.Coy. Firing was done at Enemy Aircraft attempting to cross our line. During the night, and also by day when possible much work was done on gun positions. Positions manned F.14.d were camouflaged. At F.14.d 4500 Anti Aircraft Harassing was completed. 150 yds of Trench was cleared at F.15.C.1.0. Baby Elephant shelters were put were placed in position at F.21.c.2537 as shelter for S.A.A. At F.21.d.1085 Baby Elephant shelters were dug in places at F.31.d. 10.85. and camouflaged, and also at timbered. At F.22.c.2390 trenches from dugout to gun positions were dug and camouflaged. B.Coy Shelters at E.28.c 3090 were improved. Dugouts at E.22.d. 1560, Emplacements at E.22.d. 15.35. and E.22.b. 3090, were improved. Camouflage constructed at E.21.b. 7095. C. Coy During the night 11,000 rounds were fired at the following targets L.9.c. 85.25. L.9.c. 3550. Track F.29.c.1065 to F.29.c. 6080. Wood in L.4.c. and Tracks F.27.a. 9050 to F.29.c 9025. 2000 Rounds were also fired at Enemy Aircraft. Field of fire emplacements were improved at F.30.A 8050. Trench revetted for 6 yds. at F.30.a. At F.27.a. 6080 tunnel was extended 4ftr 2ft and revetted. R.E's assisted in making Dug out at F.25.D 4599. New work was continued under R.E's on Dug outs at F.13.c.3500. Timber salved for Mn. Emplacements at F.19.a. New emplacements made at F.19.a. central and F.19.a. 4253 ammenities. Emplacement at F.19.a. 2055 continued. Propaganda. Two copies of a letter to Germans were picked up in our lines. There were evidently dropped by our Aviator.	303

Army Form C. 2118.

WAR DIARY
or
INTELLIGENCE SUMMARY.
(Erase heading not required.)

MAY

Instructions regarding War Diaries and Intelligence Summaries are contained in F. S. Regs., Part II. and the Staff Manual respectively. Title pages will be prepared in manuscript.

Place	Date	Hour	Summary of Events and Information	Remarks and references to Appendices
BUCQUOY SECTOR	5 May		Artillery on both sides fairly quiet by day but very much livelier at night. Enemy Artillery shelled the following areas. E.28.b, F.17.a, F.24.d, E.28.d, F.22.c, F.26.d, F.27.a, L.1 and L.2. Our artillery shelled ridge behind ARLAINZEVELLE very heavily. Visibility low till noon then higher. **BALLOONS** ENEMY One up on right of BUCQUOY, intermittently, but taken down when shelled. Visibility Until h.g.o. turned edwards. F.36.b and F.27.a. F.25.d and F.27.a. **MACHINE GUNS** A Coy. Work has been continued at all gun positions, and new positions – shell hole emplacements have been commenced at all guns. New positions – shell hole emplacements have been commenced at all guns. Rain & darkness hindered work a great deal. B. Coy. Have worked on their emplacements and carried out general improvements. C. Coy. Fired 11,000 rounds on the following targets. E.26.b.57.99. F.20.a.9.4.Y.3. Rail 86 + L.8a: L.4.c.7.9. — L.4.d.99.01. L.9.c.85.25. Front L.a.b.94.22 - L.4.a.5.3 Track L.a.5.5 to L.4.a.0.0. 1000 Rds were fired at Enemy Air Craft. Work has been continued at dug outs, and emplacements. New latrines have been built at L.1.D.4.6 and F.20.a.9.4. D. Coy. Dug outs at F.13.c.35.00 continued. Work done on emplacement at F.19.a. central. F.19.a.42.03 and F.19.a.25.75. Alternative position made at F.20.a.00.55. Dug out finished at F.13.c.65.00 finish improved at E.30.a.2.1.	
BUCQUOY SECTOR	6 May		Visibility which was lost in the morning, improved towards the afternoon. There was a little aeroplane activity on the part of the enemy by day, but planes were easily turned. Three light bombs were dropped in F.25.c at 7.30 p.m. Our Artillery was active during the 24 hours and answered an S.O.S. call on our left at 10 p.m. Enemy Artillery was also active on our left sector, and PRUSSIAN AVENUE in F.21.c, F.27.b was heavily shelled by gas and shrapnel during the morning. Other localities shelled were F.26, F.27. L.1 and L.2. Heavy T.M's were also sent over into L.2. There was a little activity on our left sector in F.21.c, F.27.b which was heavily shelled.	SUTR

Army Form C. 2118.

WAR DIARY
or
INTELLIGENCE SUMMARY.
(Erase heading not required.)

MAY

Instructions regarding War Diaries and Intelligence Summaries are contained in F. S. Regs., Part II. and the Staff Manual respectively. Title pages will be prepared in manuscript.

Place	Date	Hour	Summary of Events and Information	Remarks and references to Appendices
BUCQUOY SECTOR	6 MAY		Enemy Machine Guns fired around F25d. F29a. F26b. F31a and E80a+b during the night. Balloons were up behind BUCQUOY and in direction of PUISIEUX during the day. S.O.S. signal at 10 p.m.	
			A Coy. fired 6000 rds. on S.O.S line in F23a on response to S.O.S signal at 10 p.m. Work was greatly hindered by rain but the following was done. Camouflage completed at F14.B.L. Continued Camouflaging at F14.d.4.50b. F15.c.1.0. Work was continued on supports F21c.2.532. Work was continued but not much could be done because of rain.	
			B Coy. Work proceeded on emplacements at E28.c.2.9. E28c.3.9. E22b.10.10. E28d.15.35. E22b.20.90. and E21b.90.95. Two new gun positions commenced at E28.6.73.15. and E27.c.10.60.	
			C Coy. fired 7000 rounds at the following targets. Road L40.7.9.6. L4 D5.3: Roads L96. 7086 h L 96. 3.3. Road L96. 50.90. 1150 rounds were fired at enemy planes. Work was done on the following localities. L1A.4075. Trench emplacement made. F25d. 45.99. L2a 3580 Dug out improved. L1d.a.6 new emplacement worked on. F20.6. R.E.s assisted in this work. Trench has also been improved and entrance dug. 6090 definite front gun emplacement.	
		D Coy. 60 Rounds were fired at E.A. Work was continued under M.R.E's and trenches have been drained. Alternative emplacement at F20.a.0055 worked on. New S.E. emplacement commenced at E30.b.75.70.	
			Casualties. 3 O.R's wounded by shell.	
BUCQUOY SECTOR	7th MAY		The night of 6/7th was very wet, as was the morning of the 7th. Weather during the day was bad, but towards evening it became lighter.	
			Artillery. There was very am active during the night carrying out harassing fire. F29a. L13.c. F25d and F26. F20 a was also shelled during the morning. The enemy shelled the following points F29a. L13.c. F25d and F26. F20 a was also shelled during the morning.	
			Aircraft. Enemy aircraft became active + came over our lines. They were very engaged by our guns on A.A. work were driven back.	
			Balloons. Ours reported on our sector. F27a 55.85 +F26. 6090. Also E30 a+b. Enemy horizon. F27a 55.85 +F26. 6090. Also E30 a+b.	
			Machine guns.	

Army Form C. 2118.

WAR DIARY
INTELLIGENCE SUMMARY. MAY
(Erase heading not required.)

Place	Date	Hour	Summary of Events and Information	Remarks and references to Appendices
BUCQUOY SECTOR	7"		"A" Coy. 500 rounds were fired at aircraft. Work was continued at all the emplacements, and damage done to the trenches & dug-outs by the heavy rain was repaired.	
			"B" Coy. Carried out work of improvement in trenches, and at the emplacements, and commenced preliminary emplacements at E.28.c.16.90. E.27.d.50.70. E.22.d.10.30. and E.21.d.85.55.	
			"C" Coy. Carried out work on emplacements and on trenches damaged by rain. 1500 rounds were fired at enemy A/Craft and in addition the following targets were engaged. 1000 rounds being fired. Road L.8.b. & L.8.a. L.14.b.5.5. & L.3.d. 9.1 - these latter was done on observation with infantry in the raids. - Tracks in L.14.c. Road in L.14.b.	
			"D" Coy. fired 50 rounds at an enemy plane. Work was continued on emplacements and on dug-outs. A new dug-out was commenced at F.19.a.6.6. The alternative emplacements all nearing completion.	
			Casualties 10 O.R. wounded gas.	
BUCQUOY SECTOR	8"		OPERATIONS At 2p.m. two companies of the R.B. advanced their line of post in the neighbourhood of the CRUCIFIX at L.14.a.3.85, but they had to withdraw from this in the evening.	
			ARTILLERY Enemy artillery shelled intermittently during morning PIGEON WOOD and QUESNOY FARM but in the afternoon he shelled the sector very heavily with all calibres & with gas. He put down a barrage of 7.7cm on F.37.a. & a barrage of 10.5cm along railway in F.27.c. Our artillery was active during the whole gas hours.	
			Aircraft. Some enemy aircraft came over our lines in the afternoon & again in the evening & were heavily engaged by our A.A. guns. Two were driven down.	
			Machine Guns. Harassed E.30.a.15. F.27.a. & F.20.b during the night. Our guns were active during the day & night.	

Army Form C. 2118.

WAR DIARY
or
INTELLIGENCE SUMMARY. MAY

(Erase heading not required.)

Place	Date MAY	Hour	Summary of Events and Information	Remarks and references to Appendices
BUCQUOY SECTOR	6"		"A" Coy. Worked on their emplacements & further improvements until dark. 150 Rounds were fired on enemy at 1700x at 8 p.m. at E.A. at 7.30 p.m. 2000 rounds were fired on enemy at 1700x at 8 p.m. 5000 rounds were fired on road from F.23.a.90.70 to F.17.a.10.10. S.O.S. lines from Midnight till 3 A.M. 5000 rounds were fired on Target F.24.c.05.90 - F.24.c.10.12. "B" Coy. Further emplacements and trenches in their neighbourhood. "C" Coy. Fired 1550 rounds at E.A. and during the night the Road L.42.B.6 - L.10 A.2.7. was searched, 5000 rounds being fired. "D" Coy. Fired 50 rounds at an enemy plane, and continued work on their positions & emplacements. S.H.Q at F.13.d.0.3 Had a 'phone installed. Casualties 1 O.R. wounded (gas).	J.D.H
BUCQUOY SECTOR	9"		The day was very much quieter on our sector - the enemy's Artillery being less active. Our Artillery remained by day, but towards dusk is became more active. The enemy Aircraft were also much more active, several low flying machines being over our lines during the day. There were all heavily engaged by our Machine Guns. Our aeroplanes were also active + at night several bombing planes crossed the enemy lines. A Coy carried on improvements on their positions and trenches. B Coy also carried out improvements also. 1250 rounds were fired at Enemy Aircraft. C Coy. Improving existing trenches, made two new emplacements at L1A 45.55, and in addition 7500 rounds were fired at B.A. 11,750 rounds were fired on the following targets during the night. L9.D.4.a - L9.D.8.2; 3,750 rds. L9.B.8.0.80. 2,500 rds. L9.C.10.68. 3500 rds. 2 rds. L39.70.25 300 rounds. D. Coy. Also improved positions, worked on tunnels under R.E's as before. In addition Lay fired 1200 rounds at enemy flares. Enemy machine gun harassed E.30.a to F.20.B + F.27.a during the night. Casualties N.L.	E.V.B.

Army Form C. 2118.

WAR DIARY or INTELLIGENCE SUMMARY. MAY.

(Erase heading not required.)

Instructions regarding War Diaries and Intelligence Summaries are contained in F. S. Regs., Part II. and the Staff Manual respectively. Title pages will be prepared in manuscript.

Place	Date	Hour	Summary of Events and Information	Remarks and references to Appendices
BUCQUOY SECTOR	10th		The day passed fairly quietly on our front, not much activity being shewn by the enemy. Enemy artillery was quieter on the whole, and though the usual areas E.30A.4.3, E.18.C, E.24.C & L.1.D, L.2.D & L.2.C were shelled the shelling was very much lighter. Enemy planes and men our positions, but were back on being engaged. Enemy Machine Guns were active during night traversing E.30A.6, E.21.C and L.1.D, L.2.C. BALLOONS one seen at bearing of 1320° M from F.14.d.5.5. "A" Coy. fired 8000 rounds on Road F.24.c.0590 — F.25.10.12. 250 rounds were fired at enemy aircraft at F.15.C.1.0. 40' of trench were deepened and a place for a shelter made. Camouflage was erected at positions in F.14.d. "B" Coy. did a little work on their emplacements and they relief bathed at Advanced Divisional Baths at FONQUEVILLERS. "C" Coy. 1250 rounds at enemy aircraft, and fired 8,500 rounds at the following targets L.H.6.0.6, L.9.18.8.8, L.4.C.9.7, Road L.9.6.50.90. They worked on their emplacements. "D" Coy. worked on emplacements and also on tunnels under R.E.'s. Casualties Nil.	302
BUCQUOY SECTOR	11th		The day was considerably quieter in our sector, and the enemy artillery shewed a considerable increase in activity, and the forward areas of our sector were heavily shelled. He turning the enemy shelled FONQUEVILLERS for from .... with gas and high explosives. Aircraft Hostile Aircraft shewed some activity flying over BUCQUOY, BIEZ WOOD in the afternoon. In the evening at 6pm our flew over PURPLE LINE and was heavily engaged by our M.G's and Lewis Guns. Enemy machine guns traverse PRUSSIAN AVENUE in F.21.C, F.26.A, F.25.D, F.26.A.B, F.27.A, L.1.D during the night.	

WAR DIARY
INTELLIGENCE SUMMARY. MAY

Army Form C. 2113.

Place	Date	Hour	Summary of Events and Information	Remarks and references to Appendices
BUCQUOY SECTOR.	11th		"A" Coy. Finished off new emplacements at PM.B. 10.55 and put new baby elephant shelters in. Targets were engaged during the night as follows F.24.c.05.90 Road Junction. L.4.b.30.62 - L.4.b.70.30 reached and L.4.b.70.30 - L.5.a.05.00 reached 8000 rounds were fired.	
			"B" Coy. This day suffered most severely from the gun shelling on this date. 1 Officer 2/Lt G.H.CHRISTIAN and 14 O.Rs being gassed. Work was carried on an emplacement in the forenoon and afternoon.	
			"C" Coy. Fired 900 Rounds at aircraft and in addition 14,530 Rounds were fired on the following targets ROAD-RAIL JUNCTIONS L.5.D.70.85. L.9.B.76.82. L.10.A.50.60. L.3.D.60.27 - L.3.D.90.10. L.4.A.80.83. L.4.c.70.90. and L.4.c.41.55. Work was carried out as usual improving shelters + sandbagging a new Amty. Pad at F.25.D.80.50. Trenches were also improved.	
			"D" Coy. Moved guns etc to new Position at F.19.c.42.53. Other emplacements were worked on and tunnelling was carried out under R.E.A.	D.O.B.
			Casualties 2/Lt CHRISTIAN P.B. "B" Coy and 15 O.Rs were wounded by Gas. 3 O.Rs were wounded , one of whom was able remain at duty.	
BUCQUOY SECTOR.	12th		The day was quieter on the whole than the previous day in this sector. Enemy Artillery showed normal activity, shelling the following areas. FONQUEVILLERS with 10·5 c.m. shells and also sending over 16 gas shellers in forenoon. Other areas shelled were F.19.c. L.20. L.13. F.19.B. E.10.A and E.30. Enemy Machine guns harrassed the usual positions from dusk until dawn, but his fire was not very heavy during this night.	

(A7092). Wt. W23530/M1293 75,10,0, 1/17. D. D. & L., Ltd. Forms/C.2118/14.

Army Form C. 2118.

WAR DIARY
or
INTELLIGENCE SUMMARY.

MAY

(Erase heading not required.)

Place	Date	Hour	Summary of Events and Information	Remarks and references to Appendices
BUCQUOY SECTOR	10		Visibility was low during the forenoon, but later it improved. Enemy aircraft were active in the evening several being seen and forward areas between 6 pm & 7.30. All were engaged by M.G's and came over people line about 8.30 were engaged 1,550 rounds were fired at them. Our aircraft were also active and a number crossed the enemy lines in the evening returning by night and bombing parties. There was much as usual, but when our planes crossed at night enemy sent up a white parachute light which remained in the air for some months. Flare lights were seen when enemy were near ABLAINZEVELLES 11.15 p.m.	
			Bellum. H.Up opposite our sector between 5.7 pm & 6.30 p.m.	
			A Coy. fired 340 rounds at enemy aircraft and fired 8000 rounds on F.5A/c 05.90 - A 29a 10.10. L.46.36.62 - L.46.70.50. L.46.70.30 - L.5a.05.00. but was carried on at F.15C.10 and on general improvements	
			B Coy. carried on improving emplacements and trenches until this work was not carried on to much an extent because of the recent gas shelling in this vicinity	
			C Coy. carried on their trench improvements on fortress and shelters. The Coy fired 1200 rounds at E.A) ank find 1100 rounds by night on the following targets L.10a.70.65. Road L.9.6.76.62. Trench L.6d.60.27. L.5d 90.10 trench Road function L.10.a.5.10. Dump L.L.a. H.155. L.2C.8.9 L2 u.a. 9.5.	
			D Coy. Completed new emplacement at F19c Central. F19W42.53. Work was carried out	
			CASUALTIES: 5 O.R's ISHELL 4GAS	

Army Form C. 2118.

WAR DIARY
or
INTELLIGENCE SUMMARY.
(Erase heading not required.)

MAY

Place	Date	Hour	Summary of Events and Information	Remarks and references to Appendices
BUCQUOY SECTOR	MAY 13.		The general situation was unchanged. Enemy artillery showed great activity over the left of our sector and on the right of the sector on our immediate left. Less shelling is reported from our other groups. Areas shelled were F.28, F.15a+b, F.21, E.15a, E.15b, K.4b, E.11c, PIGEON WOOD, E.29b, E.20, L.1A+B, L.2, L.3A, F.25, E.30, B.12 WOOD, ESSARTS and F.13c. Our artillery was fairly active, but no more so than usual. Enemy A/craft were very active in the early morning as many as ten being reported over our lines on the Right sector JJ. Left sector at 6 a.m. Over the right sector from intervals from 6 - 11 a.m. enemy machines were busy. Our Aeroplanes were also active all morning and during the night 12/13. They were also active.	
			Balloons. 6 - 9 a.m. 2 am bearing 145° and 160° grid from F.26 a 85.50. 5.30 - 10 a.m. 3 am bearing 120°, 130° and 160° " "	
			Enemy machine guns carried out usual harassing fire during the night.	
			A Coy. carried out improvements as already reported. This included clearing of trenches + improvements of emplacements. Forming troughs 5000 rounds were fired on the following trgts. Road Junction F.30 a 15.60, F.30 a 35.32. Bus F.24 a Central Road F.29 b 90.90 and F.24 c 50.90.	
			B.Coy. Commenced work on extension at E.29a 35.70, and continued work at E.21 a 95.35, a new alternative front in windmill at E.28 a 50.70.	
			C Coy. Continued improvements carried in making dug outs at F.25d 45.99 & F.25d 50.99 with R.E.'s. At F.27 a 55.85, a tunnel was being driven another front. L.8d 80.85, L.9b 96.62, L.4d 61.14, L.4c 48.20 and L.4B. 9000 rounds were fired at L.8d 80.85, L.9b 96.62, L.4d 61.14, L.4c 48.20 and L.4B 5.5.	

Army Form C. 2113.

WAR DIARY
INTELLIGENCE SUMMARY. MAY.
(Erase heading not required.)

Instructions regarding War Diaries and Intelligence Summaries are contained in F. S. Regs., Part II. and the Staff Manual respectively. Title pages will be prepared in manuscript.

Place	Date	Hour	Summary of Events and Information	Remarks and references to Appendices
RUCQUOY SECTOR	13th		"A" Bery. fired 300 rounds at Enemy Aircraft, and continued tunnelling under R.E.8. at F19C.6.6 & F.25a 45.80. Work was done at Emplacement at E24C 80.81. CASUALTIES. NIL--	
	14th		The enemy artillery showed more activity today, and at times shelling was very heavy. Areas shelled were E 29, E 30, F 25, F 19, L1 and L 2. Hostile Aircraft showed more than usual activity over the right sector. They were twice engaged by our machine gun. 3,050 rounds being fired. Our guns were also active both day & night. 6 B alarms were sent up at various times at 2 gun bearings 103°, 110° 115° 125° 140° and 145° from E 21d 9505. The enemy carried out his usual harassing fire during the night. Church cut emplacements were made good. Damage done by rain a by. When drilling and shelling they fired At the following targets during the night. Battery F19C.6.1.=296 O.S. Cross Roads F.23d.40.55 and Valley F18A. Guns rounds were fired on these targets & 300 at E.4.	
			B Coy. Commenced an enlargement at E 9 c o. 35.00 + another at E 22 c 25.03. Work was resumed at other places where the Previous T.S.es had finished.	
			C Coy. Fired during the night on the following targets L4a sheeter, Rabobo in L9 b Trenches in L10a Ram 66 rc Valley in 9a central. 9 000 rounds were fired in addition 2300 rounds were fired at E A. Work on tunnelling was continued and New enlargements occured at E 24 C 80. 81 + Work 450 rounds under R E B continued.	
			D Coy. 24 C 81. Work under R E 8 continued. Casualties Nil.	

Army Form C. 2118.

WAR DIARY
or
INTELLIGENCE SUMMARY.   MAY.

(Erase heading not required.)

Place	Date	Hour	Summary of Events and Information	Remarks and references to Appendices
BUCQUOY SECTOR	MAY 15		Artillery Activity was considerable on both sides, and the day was very favourable for good observation. The usual localities were shelled with all calibres. The enemy made use of shrapnel more today than usual. His Artillery was active by day and very much so by night.	
			Aerial Activity was also great owing to the good weather, and one hostile aeroplane bomb on our front line near BUCQUOY. Our Aircraft were also very busy during the 24 hours, several machines bombing the enemy at night.	
			Machine Gun activity on the part of the enemy was about normal, the usual harassing fire being maintained.	
			Balloons. Several enemy balloons were up at intervals during the morning and evening.	
			A Coy. At F.15.c.1.0 about 50 yds. of trenches were cleaned, and shelter emplacements were worked on. More camouflage was used. Next potatoes were crept over with soda. During the night the following targets were engaged: Centres of Movement at F.34.a.1.0. Tramway in F.29.6. Posts/Movement Areas in F.23.6, and 25.a. 8000 rounds were fired on these targets and 1300 rounds at E.A.	
			B. Coy. At E.22.0.10.10 Obstructions were placed in trenches near positions, and work was continued at emplacement at E.22.0.10.40 + E.21.d.90.60.	
			C. Coy. Work was continued at the Tunnel in F.29.A. New positions made at F.27.A.53.85 and F.25.D.53.00. Dug out making continued at L.4.A & L.4.C. Tracks and Roads in L.8.d & L.9.6. New post at L.5.a.1. Movement areas in L.4.A. 2250 Rounds were fired at Enemy Aircraft.	
			D. Coy. Continued work with R.E.s at F.19.c.46. + F.25.a.45.00 alternative Emplacements. Has worked on at F.19.a. F.13.c. 60.15 and F.13.c. 7.3.	
			Casualties Nil.	

WAR DIARY or INTELLIGENCE SUMMARY.

Army Form C. 2118.

MAY.

(Erase heading not required.)

Place	Date	Hour	Summary of Events and Information	Remarks and references to Appendices
BUCQUOY SECTOR	MAY 16		**Artillery.** – Enemy Artillery was again fairly lively & a few gas shells were fired into FONQUEVILLERS. The usual areas were shelled. Our Artillery also was active and shelled enemy support line very heavily.	
			Aircraft. – Enemy Aircraft were active in considerable force the night action of our front & a few machines flew over our lines FONQUEVILLERS. Our machines displayed usual activity and were machines than usual crossed enemy lines at night.	
			Balloons. 6 were up at intervals during day at True Bearings 102°; 110°; 115°; 125°; 142°;148° from E 28 a 25.45.	
			Machine Gun Activity on the part of the enemy was slightly more increased, guns in ABLAINZEVELLE being exceptionally active.	
			"A" Coy. Infantry trenches in neighbourhood of F.15.c.10. and made shelters for Lewis teams at the same place.	
			The following targets were engaged. Area F.29 a & F.23 b 7.0 & thereabouts. Area L.4.b. and F.29 a 0072. These areas were searched & traversed. 500 Rounds fired at E.A.	
			"B" Coy. Pulled a dug out at E 22 c 7.4 and worked on emplacements at E 22 c 1.1. E 28 a 50 35. & E 28 a 4.4. 100 Rounds fired at E.A.	
			"C" Coy. Worked on tunnels at F.17 A and on emplacements in F.29 a & 29 c. 1. F 20 d 5209. R.E.s carried to make dug out at F.25.D. Work was also done on other positions – general improvements being carried out. 8500 Rounds were fired during the night ready entering on the following target beings – Roads L.4.a. Road Tracks L.4.a & L.4.c. Tracks L.9a & L.9d. Trenches in L.8. and L.9. These roads were well searched. 100 Rounds fired at E.A.	
			"D" Coy. – Continued tunnelling at F19a 6 6 & F25 a 45 80. and the trench in F19a blocked by wire. 450 Rounds fired at E.A.	
			Casualties 3850 Corporal PORTEOUS B. Coy. Killed.	

Army Form C. 2118.

WAR DIARY
INTELLIGENCE SUMMARY.
MAY

(Erase heading not required.)

Place	Date	Hour	Summary of Events and Information	Remarks and references to Appendices
BUCQUOY SECTOR	14th		Today was fairly lively on our front, and Artillery activity was fairly great. The usual areas were shelled but it was noticeable that today the enemy burst his black shrapnel much lower than usual.	
			Aircraft. In both sides aerial activity after the morning mist lifted, and one plane was seen to crash about L 8 A. Enemy machine low however without hilly made sights today than usual.	
			Machine Gun Activity was about normal on the part of the enemy F 20 A being particularly selected as a target.	
			Balloons. 9 were seen at various intervals. Our planes attacked one forcing the occupant to leave it.	
			"A" Coy. The company was relieved by D Company, 62nd Infy. Bns. Relief was complete at 11.30 p.m. + the Coy arrived at BOIS DU WARNIMONT 1.17.C (Ref 2000 FRANCE SHEET 57 D.N.W) at 4.30 A.M. Lorries were provided from SOUASTRE. In anticipation of our being relieved L 4 was heavily strafed and then target was handed over to the relieving Company.	
			"B" Coy. The Coy was relieved on the line by "C" Coy 62" M.G. Bn. Relief complete at 7 p.m. Coy reached BOIS D.U. WARNIMONT at	
			"C" Coy. In anticipation of heavy relief in sight L 9 and L 10 all night. It is was discharged 13,750 rounds being fired. Work on positions was carried on as before.	
			"D" Coy. Tunnelling continued under R.E. Trench at F.19 a central blocked by wire.	
			CASUALTIES One man wounded.	

Army Form C. 2118.

WAR DIARY
or
INTELLIGENCE SUMMARY.
(Erase heading not required.)

Instructions regarding War Diaries and Intelligence Summaries are contained in F. S. Regs., Part II. and the Staff Manual respectively. Title pages will be prepared in manuscript.

Place	Date	Hour	Summary of Events and Information	Remarks and references to Appendices
HENU	17.		The Battalion at 9 p.m. Bn. Headquarters will remain at HENU & BOIS DU WARNIMONT at	Appendix I
AUTHIE			AUTHIE. Battalion H.Q. opened at 1.17 d. 1535 Ref. 1/2000 FRANCE SHEET 57D NW. TRANSPORT lines were opened at 1.17 c 9.7.	
			A Coy details with Transport and B Coy details with Transport moved from HENU to BOIS DU WARNIMONT in the afternoon to-day	2nd Lt
BUCQUOY SECTOR.	18.		In the line to-day Enemy Artillery was active over visual areas carrying out harassing fire. Aerial activity was also great to-day both sides continuing active.	
			"C" Coy of 37" Mdy. Bn. was relieved in the line by "A" Coy 62" Bn. Mdy.Bn. Relief was completed at 9.45 p.m. The Company was conveyed from SOUASTRE to BOIS DU WARNIMONT by lorries and reached camp at 1.30 a.m. 19."	
			Lt. A.S. PULLEY joined the Company from BASE DEPOT to-day.	
			D. Coy was relieved in the line by "B" Company 62" Mdy. Bn. Relief was completed at	
BOIS DU			and the Company arrived in Camp at BOIS DU WARNIMONT at 12.30 a.m. 19."	
WARNIMONT				

Army Form C. 2118.

WAR DIARY
or
INTELLIGENCE SUMMARY. MAY.

(Erase heading not required.)

Instructions regarding War Diaries and Intelligence Summaries are contained in F. S. Regs., Part II. and the Staff Manual respectively. Title pages will be prepared in manuscript.

Place	Date	Hour	Summary of Events and Information	Remarks and references to Appendices
Bois DU WARNIMONT	19.		"A" Coy picked and cleaned up after coming out of the line. Bows and gun kit were thoroughly overhauled and cleaned later on the day. The Company had baths & May and a change of clothing.	
ORVILLE			"B" Coy. Proceeded from BOIS DU WARNIMONT to ORVILLE where they trained and commenced rifle firing on the ranges there.	
BOIS DU WARNIMONT			"C" Coy bathed, and were refitted in the afternoon. The remainder of the day was spent cleaning arms & equipment. O.C. Coy walked H.Q. 112 Infy Bgde.	
			"D" Coy also bathed and rested after checking & cleaning arms & gun kit and equipment.	9pps.
BOIS DU	20.		The battalion less "B" Coy commenced a programme of training which was chalked out for into each advanced new syllabus. Firing was done on the short range in I.17.a.Part	
WARNIMONT			I to the C.being fired. "B" Coy trained at ORVILLE. Afternoon spent in recreational training	
ORVILLE			"B" Coy carried out training and Range Practice.	
BOIS DU	21.		The battalion less "B" Company continued its training according to programme laid down. Table 7J 9pps.	
WARNIMONT			Firing was done on the short range — recreational training done in afternoon.	
ORVILLE			"B" Coy carried out training and rifle firing	9pps.

Army Form C. 2118.

WAR DIARY
or
INTELLIGENCE SUMMARY.
(Erase heading not required.)

Instructions regarding War Diaries and Intelligence Summaries are contained in F. S. Regs., Part II. and the Staff Manual respectively. Title pages will be prepared in manuscript.

Place	Date	Hour	Summary of Events and Information	Remarks and references to Appendices
BOIS DU WARNIMONT	22		A, C, & D Companies hutt spent this morning in a G defence with the Infantry Brigades of the Division, manning the Red Line. On receipt of "Practice BATTLE POSITIONS" A Coy moved off in 30 minutes, C Coy 55 minutes, D Coy 50 minutes. The whole Battalion "Stood to" whole practice was carried out and in the afternoon usual normal conditions. S.B.R's were worn at work for one hour.	
ORVILLE			B Coy threw live grenades and fired Rifle grenades. Field firing also was carried out.	Appx/3
BOIS du WARNIMONT	23		"B" Coy returned march over dislodge of "C" Coy in Corps Reserve. C Coy proceeded ORVILLE for training and field firing. A & D Companies carried on with training as per programme. RESPIRATORS worn for 1 hour.	Appendix II 7/3
ORVILLE			"C" Coy at ORVILLE training and on the range.	7/3
BOIS DU WARNIMONT	24		Commanding Officer lectured all Officers on lessons from Recent fighting after which A & B carried on with training as per programme. "B" Coy relieved "D" Coy in the N.Z.M.G. Posn in the PURPLE LINE RIGHT DIVISIONAL SECTOR. Map reference of Posn. REF FRANCE SHEET 57D N.E. 2 guns K8d 6.6. 2 guns K 14b 1.1. 1 gun at K14c 1.3. 1 gun at K14c 1.3. 2 guns at K13d 75.15. 2 guns at K19c 5.F.	Appendix III 7/3
ORVILLE	24		C Coy continued their training at ORVILLE. Respirators worn for one hour.	Appx/3
BOIS DU WARNIMONT	25		A, B & 2 Sections of D Coy continued training as per programme. Respirator worn for one hour.	Appx/3
ORVILLE	25		C Coy continued training and field firing.	Appx/3
CAILLY au BOIS SECTOR	25		Two Sections of D Company in the PURPLE LINE	

WAR DIARY or INTELLIGENCE SUMMARY.

Army Form C. 2118.

MAY.

(Erase heading not required.)

Instructions regarding War Diaries and Intelligence Summaries are contained in F. S. Regs., Part II. and the Staff Manual respectively. Title pages will be prepared in manuscript.

Place	Date	Hour	Summary of Events and Information	Remarks and references to Appendices
SAILLY AU BOIS SECTOR	26		Gas Sections in Purple Line. D Coy CASUALTIES NIL	EOR
BOIS DU WARNIMONT			A. B. & D Sections of B Company will be billeted here. Clean change then after cleaning up Respirators worn 1 hour	
ORVILLE			C Coy continued training at ORVILLE	
SAILLY AU BOIS	27		2 Sections D Coy in Purple Line. Remainder of Company moved to BUS LES ARTOIS CASUALTIES NIL	EOR
ORVILLE			C Coy went through live Grenade throwing. 15 Coys Commanders interviewed new Area during the afternoon	
BOIS DU WARNIMONT			A. B. Companies continued musketry training as per programme.	
BOIS DU WARNIMONT	28		C Coy returned to Camp the morning & came under orders of G.O.C. 111th Brigade.	Operation II EOR
			B Coy continued Musketry training according to programme.	
ORVILLE			A Coy proceeded to ORVILLE at 5 A.M. this morning & commenced training & field firing.	Operation II
SAILLY AU BOIS			2 Sections of B Coy a remainder 8 Sections at BUS.	
SAILLY AU BOIS	29		2 Sections in Purple Line. Remainder two sections of D Coy in BUS Casualties NIL	EOR
ORVILLE			A Coy were in the range field firing at ORVILLE	
BOIS DU WARNIMONT			B & C Coys continued training here as per programme. One Section of C Coy did a return with 10" R.F.	
SAILLY AU BOIS	30		2 Sections of D Coy in Purple Line. Remainder of Company at BUS. Casualties Nil	EOR
ORVILLE			A Coy did training with Lewis Gun and Lewis Gun & Tank Crossed. A Coy trained afternoon & evening	
BOIS DU WARNIMONT			G.O.C. IV Corps today inspected B & C Coys with all Transport and was witnessed a tactical attack done by B Coy of C Company. Remainder of Day found training as per programme	

Army Form C. 2118.

WAR DIARY
INTELLIGENCE SUMMARY.
(Erase heading not required.)

Place	Date	Hour	Summary of Events and Information	Remarks and references to Appendices
SAILLY au BOIS	31.		To-day "B" Company relieved "D" Company two sections of "C" taking over the positions two sections of "B" now holding in the Purple line. The remaining two sections took over from the two sections stationed at BUS. "D" Company returned to BOIS DU WARNIMONT on completion of relief and both are accommodation vacated by "B" Coy.	Appendix 7
BOIS DU WARNIMONT	31.		"B" Coy trained as per programme	202
ORVILLE	31.		"A" Coy continued training and field firing	202
				202

F.J. Burdin Lieut-Col.
Commanding 37th Bn. Machine Gun. Corps.

WAR DIARY or INTELLIGENCE SUMMARY. MAY

Army Form C. 2118.

(Erase heading not required.)

Place	Date	Hour	Summary of Events and Information	Remarks and references to Appendices
			The following changes in the furnish of the Battalion took place during the month	
			Lt. Col. E.D. BASDEN. M.C. took command on MAY 11.	
			Lt. Col. W.V.L. PRESCOTT-WESTCARR. D.S.O. relinquished command 10. MAY	
			The following officers joined as Reinforcements during the month.	
			CAPTAIN GILSHENAN T.S.	
			LIEUT. SARGENT C.G.	
			LIEUT. PULLEY A.S.	
			LIEUT. MOLE G.H.	
			LIEUT. JUST J.C.	
			The following Officers were evacuated.	
			2/Lt. CHRISTIAN WOUNDED GAS	
			2/Lt. FALCONER	
			2/Lt. OLIVER H.D. SICK.	
			The following O.R's joined the Battalion during the month as reinforcements	
			18" May 78 O.R's 25" May 6 O.R's	
			24" May 30 O.R's 28" May 29 O.R's	

T.F. Sadler Lieut.-Col.
Commanding 37th Bn. Machine Gun. Corps.

SECRET.　　　37TH BATTALION MACHINE GUN CORPS.　　COPY NO. 17

OPERATION ORDER NO 28.

REF. MAPS. 1/20,000. SHEET 57 D.N.E.　　　　　　　　15TH MAY/1918.
　　　　　　1/40,000. SHEET 57 D.

1. The Division (less Artillery) will be relieved by the 62nd Division (less Artillery) on the night of the 16th/17th May.

2. On the night of the 16th/17th May the 63rd Infantry Brigade will be relieved by the 186th Infantry Brigade.
On the night of the 17th/18th May the 112th Infantry Brigade will be relieved by the 185th Infantry Brigade, and the 111th Infantry Brigade will be relieved by 187th Infantry Brigade.

3. The 63rd Brigade and one Machine Gun Company will be at the disposal of G.O.C. N.Z. Division for counter-attack purposes from 12 noon 17th May 1918.
"A" Coy. 62nd B'n. M.G.C. (I.17.d.central) will be at the disposal of the G.O.C. 63rd Infantry Brigade from 12 noon 17th inst to 9.a.m. 18th inst. The Company Commander will report to H.Q. 63rd Infantry Brigade at 9.a.m. 17th inst.
"A" Coy. 37th B'n. M.G.C. will relieve "A" Coy. 62nd B'n. M.G.C. at 9.a.m. 18th inst. The Company Commander will report Brigade H.Q. at this hour.

4. The 37th B'n. M.G.C. will be relieved by 62nd B'n. M.G.C. on the nights of 17th/18th May and 18th/19th May.
Advance parties of the 62nd B'n. will be attached to corresponding Companies of 37th B'n. under arrangements to be made by Company Commanders concerned.

5. Reliefs will be carried out as follows:-
(a) On the night of the 17th/18th May
"A" Coy. 37th B'n. will be relieved by "D" Coy. 62nd B'n.
"B" Coy. (3 sections) 37th B'n. will be relieved by "C" Coy. 62nd B'n. (3 sections).
(b) On the night of the 18th/19th May
"C" Coy. 37th B'n. will be relieved by "A" Coy. 62nd B'n.
"D" Coy. 37th B'n. will be relieved by "B" Coy. 62nd B'n.
All arrangements will be made between Company Commanders concerned.

6. Details of relief of Signal Sections will be arranged by Signal Officers.

7. Trench stores; 1/10,000 and 1/20,000 maps; Intelligence Maps; and List of work in progress will be handed over.
A.P. S.A.A. will be handed over.
16 Belt Boxes per gun will be brought out.
Guns and Tripods will not be exchanged, and petrol tins will not be handed over.
Copies of Trench Store Receipts will be handed into Orderly Room by mid-day on the day following relief.

8. On relief, Companies will take over the accommodation vacated at BOIS DU WARNIMONT by the Companies relieving them. Companies and the Transport Officer will send advance parties to take over accommodation and stores.
Rear H.Q. and spare Transport of Companies will move at 2.p.m. on the day the Company is relieved.
Tents, corrugated iron and shelters will be left. Receipts for tents will be obtained.
On arrival at BOIS DU WARNIMONT Companies will be complete in Mobile Reserve of S.A.A.

9. While in Corps Reserve the Division will be at one hours notice from 9.p.m. to 9.a.m. and at two hours notice from 9.a.m. to 9.p.m.

10. Battalion Headquarters will close at HFNU at 9.p.m. 17th inst. and will open at BOIS DU VARNIMONT at the same hour.

11. Relief complete will be reported by wiring code word "DONE".

12. ACKNOWLEDGE. (Units of 37th B'n.M.G.C. only).

Issued at 10.p.m. May 15th/1918.

R H Peacock
Capt.
Adjutant 37th B'n. Machine Gun Corps.

COPIES TO:-

1. 37th. Division "G".
2. 37th. Division "Q".
3. Commanding Officer.
4. "A" Company.
5. "B"   do
6. "C"   do
7. "D"   do
8. Signal Officer
9. 62nd. B'n. M.G. Corps.
10. 63rd. Infantry Brigade.
11. 111th. Infantry Brigade.
12. 112th. Infantry Brigade.
13. T.O., Q.M., M.O.
14. C.M.G.O.
15. Guards. M.G. B'n.
16. 57th. M.G. B'n.
17) War Diary
18)
19. File.

War Diary

appendix II

SECRET.

COPY NO. 10

37TH BATTALION MACHINE GUN CORPS.

OPERATION ORDER NO 29.

22/5/18.

1. The following changes in the disposition of the 37th B'n.M.G. Corps will take place on the morning of the 23rd inst.
   "B" Coy.will move from ORVILLE to the BOIS DU WARNIMONT and take over the duties of "C" Coy.
   "C" Coy.will move to ORVILLE for purposes of training and field firing.

2. O.C. "C" Coy.will leave an Officer who will hand over and explain to O.C. "B" Coy.all duties regarding defence, counter attack schemes, etc. This Officer will be attached to "B" Coy.until the night of 23rd/24th for the purpose of showing dispositions of Machine Guns etc in the Sector taken over.
   O.C. "C" Coy.will also leave 3 guides for the gun positions for the same period.

3. The responsibility regarding Machine Gun attachment to G.O.C. 112th Infantry Brigade passes from O.C. "C" Coy. to O.C. "B" Coy at 5.a.m. 23/5/18.

4. O.C. "B" Coy. will report at 112th Brigade.H.Q. as early as possible after taking over.

5. Both Companies will move at 5.a.m.and each will take over the accommodation vacated by the other. Small advance parties will be sent the previous evening to take over.

6. Acknowledge. (Units of Battalion only).

Issued at 5.p.m. 22/5/18.

R.A.Peacock,
Capt.
Adjt.37th B'n.Machine Gun Corps.

COPIES TO:-

1. 37th Division "G".
2. 112th Infantry Brigade.
3. Commanding Officer.
4. O.C. "A" Coy.
5. O.C. "B" Coy.
6. O.C. "C" Coy.
7. O.C. "D" Coy.
8. Quartermaster.
9. Transport Officer.
10. War Diary.
11. File.

SECRET.   COPY NO. 16

Appendix III

37th BATTALION, MACHINE GUN CORPS.

24th May 1918.

OPERATION ORDER NO. 30.

Ref. Map 1/40000 Sheet 57 D.

1. The 63rd Inf. Bde. will relieve the 2nd N.Z. Inf. Bde. (H.Q. BUS LES ARTOIS) in the PURPLE LINE System Right Divisional Sector, today.

2. The 111th Inf. Bde. will cease to be at the disposal of the G.O.C. N.Z. Divn. from 12 noon 24th May and will take over the defence of the left sector of the 37th Div. Sector of the Red line as from that time.

3. 2 Sections of "D" Coy. will relieve 2 Sections N.Z. M.G. Bn. in the Northern portion of the Right Divisional PURPLE System by midnight 24/25th May.
"D" Coy. less 2 Sections will remain at BOIS DU WARNIMONT and will come under the orders of G.O.C. N.Z. Division from midnight 24/25th May onwards.

4. "D" Coy. will continue to be administered by the Battn.

5. "A" Coy. will take over the defence of the left sector of the 37th Divisional Sector of the RED Line from "D" Coy. from 12 noon 24th May.

6. Acknowledge. (M.G. Coys.)

        Issued at 11.40 a.m.   24th May 1918.

                                       (Sgd) R.H. PEACOCK,
                                               Capt. & Adjt.
                               37th Battn. Machine Gun Corps.

COPIES TO:-

1. 37th Division "G".
2. 37th Division "Q"
3. Commanding Officer.
4. "A" Company.
5. "B"   "
6. "C"   "
7. "D"   "
8. Signal Officer.
9. N.Z. Div. "G".
10. N.Z. Div. M.G. Bn.
11. 63rd Inf. Bde.
12. 111th Inf. Bde.
13. 112th Inf. Bde.
14. C.M.G.O.
15. T.O., Q.M., M.O.
16.) War Diary.
17.)
18. File.

SECRET. Appendix V COPY NO. 13

37th BATTALION. MACHINE GUN CORPS.

OPERATION ORDER NO. 32.

29th May 1918.

1. The 111th Inf. Bde. will relieve the 63rd Inf. Bde. in the PURPLE LINE System Right Divisional Sector on the night 30th/31st May 1918.

2. "C" Coy. 37th Bn. M.G.Corps will relieve "D" Coy. in the PURPLE LINE System on the night of 31st May/1st June 1918.

3. 2 Sections of "C" Coy. will take over from 2 Sections of "D" Coy. the following gun positions:-
    2 guns at K.18.d.   80 60
    2 guns at K.14.b.   10 10
    1 gun at K.14.c.   10 30
    1 gun at K.13.d.   75 15
    2 guns at K.19.c.   50 80

4. The remainder of the Company will take over the corresponding dispositions of "D" Coy.

5. Details of relief will be arranged between Company Commanders concerned.

6. On relief "D" Coy. will move to BOIS DU WARNIMONT and take over the accommodation vacated by "C" Coy. "D" Coy. will also take over all duties at present performed by "C" Coy. Respective responsibilities of O.C. "C" Coy. and O.C. "D" Coy. pass at 10 p.m. May 31st.

7. Both Companies will send advance parties 24 hours before relief.

8. All maps, orders, trench stores etc. will be handed over.

9. O.C. "D" Coy. will report to H.Q. 63rd Inf. Bde. as soon as possible after relief.

10. Completion of relief will be notified to New Zealand Battn. M.G.Corps and these Headquarters.

11. Acknowledge (M.G.Corps only)

Issued at 4 p.m.

R.A.Peacock Capt.
Adjt. 37th Battn.Machine Gun Corps.

COPIES TO:-
1. "G" 37th Division.
2. 63rd Inf.Bde.
3. 111th Inf.Bde.
4. Commanding Officer.
5. "A" Company.
6. "B" Company.
7. "C" Company.
8. "D" Company.
9. N.Z.Division "G".
10. N.Z. M.G.Battn.
11. Q.M.
12. T.O.
13.) War Diary.
14.)
15. File.

SECRET [War Diary] Appendix IV

COPY NO. 10

37TH BATTALION. MACHINE GUN CORPS.

OPERATION ORDER NO. 31.

28th May 1918.

1. The following changes in the disposition of the 37th Battn. M.G.C. will take place on Tuesday morning, 28th inst.
"C" Company will move from ORVILLE to the BOIS DE WARNIMONT and take over the duties of "A" Company.
"A" Company will move to ORVILLE for the purposes of training and field firing.

2. O.C. "A" Company will leave an officer who will hand over and explain to O.C. "C" Company all duties regarding defence, counter-attack schemes, etc. This Officer will be attached to "C" Company until the night of the 28/29th inst. for the purpose of showing dispositions of Machine Guns etc. in the sector taken over.
O.C. "A" Company will also leave 2 guides for the gun positions for the same period.

3. The responsibility regarding Machine Gun attachment to O.C. 111th Infantry Brigade passes from O.C. "A" Company to O.C. "C" Company at 6 a.m. 28th inst.

4. O.C. "C" Company will report at 111th Infantry Brigade H.Q. as early as possible after taking over.

5. Both Companies will move at 6 a.m. and each will take over the accommodation vacated by the other. Small advanced parties will be sent the previous evening to take over.

6. Acknowledge. (M.G. only)

Issued at 10 p.m.

S.H. Peacock Capt.
Adjt. 37th Bn. Machine Gun Corps.

COPIES TO:-
1. 37th Division "G".
2. 111th Infantry Brigade.
3. Commanding Officer.
4. O.C. "A" Company.
5. O.C. "B" Company.
6. O.C. "C" Company.
7. O.C. "D" Company.
8. Quartermaster.
9. Transport Officer.
10. War Diary.
11. File.

Vol 4

37th Battalion Machine Gun Corps

War Diary

month of June 1918.

WAR DIARY or INTELLIGENCE SUMMARY.

Army Form C. 2118.

JUNE 1918.

(Erase heading not required.)

Place	Date	Hour	Summary of Events and Information	Remarks and references to Appendices
BOIS du WARNIMONT	1.		"B" Company continued training as per programme of training, and also taken out a tactical operation in conjunction with "F" Pln. Coy.	
			"D" Company left BOIS du WARNIMONT and proceeded to ORVILLE to carry out training over open field firing.	Appendix I
ORVILLE			"A" Coy on completion of pln. firing and training moved from ORVILLE and occupies the favorite area vacated by D. Company.	
SAILLY au BOIS	2.		"C" Company took two sections in the PURPLE LINE RIGHT DIVISIONAL SECTOR Ref Kylcherst offensive Ref. 57D.NW. FRANCE Sheet 57D N.E. Bguns K.6.d.8.6. Bguns K.16.b.1.1. 1Gun K.14.C.1.3. 1 gun at K.13.d. 75/15. 2 guns at K.19.C.5.6. Remainder two sections with transport and establ. at BUS-LES ARTOIS.	flew/impt
BOIS de WARNIMONT			A + B Companies baths & clothes change. Remainder of day spent cleaning up.	flew/impt
ORVILLE			D. Company did field firing and training.	
SAILLY au BOIS			C. Coy had 2 sections in the PURPLE LINE and two sections at BUS.	flew/impt
Do	3.		A+B Companies trained. "D" Company did field firing "C" Coy at BUS 2 sections in Purple Line	flew/impt
Do	4.		A+B Companies trained. C Company relieved by N.Z. Bn. D Coy returned to BOIS du WARNIMONT Transport moved duck board new Arras by Road.	flew/impt

Army Form C. 2118.

WAR DIARY
of
INTELLIGENCE SUMMARY. June 1918.

(Erase heading not required.)

Instructions regarding War Diaries and Intelligence Summaries are contained in F.S. Regs., Part II, and the Staff Manual respectively. Title pages will be prepared in manuscript.

Reference Map. FRANCE AMIENS 17. CAVILLON 1B 0508. WAILLY 3B 9024.

Place	Date	Hour	Summary of Events and Information	Remarks and references to Appendices
BOIS DU HARIMONT	5		Companies standing by. at dusk moves to Embassy Road in AUTHIE THIEVES ROAD. to march to new area.	Appendix I
CAVILLON AREA	6		Companies at new area. H.Q. A Coy FOURDRINOY. B' SEUX. C' SAVEUSE. D' FERRIÈRES	
do	7		A Coy Transt. B & C Coy changed billets. B. at SAVEUSE. C. SEUX. D. and E FOURDRINOY.	
do	8		Training on lines programme. LT. T. L. TIMPERLEY joined Bn from base dept. Posted to C Coy. 8. CQMS joined	
do	9		CHURCH Parade. Coys standing by ready.	
CONDY AREA	10		Coys left CAVILLON area by Buses & arrived CONDY AREA. Bn HQ WAILLY. A Coy NEUVILLE. BCoy RUMIGNY.	Appendix III
do	11		C Coy to BOSQUEL. D Coy FLEURY.	
do	12		Coy training. Roads reconnoitred 3/Lt Prior joined unit posted to A Coy. 2/Lt Rowe joined & was posted to B Coy.	
do	13		Companies training. Further reconnaissance of roads & forward areas by Company Officers.	
do	14		Companies training. C Coy moved from le BOSQUEL to SAINS LES AMIENOIS	Appendix IV
do	15		Companies training. D Coy moved from FLEURY to NEUVILLE in the evening.	
do	16		Companies training via the evening through out following. A Coy to RUMIGNY. B Coy to SAINS LES AMIENOIS. C Coy to ST FUSCIEN. D Coy to HERECOURT. Move made under cover of night.	
do	17		Companies at work getting new quarters right, resting.	
do	18-19		All ranks working according to programme of training drawn up by O.C. Company. as on 17. Companies training	

Army Form C. 2118.

WAR DIARY
or
INTELLIGENCE SUMMARY. June 1918.

(Erase heading not required.)

Place	Date	Hour	Summary of Events and Information	Remarks and references to Appendices
CONTY AREA	19		"A" Company moved to PLACHY at midnight, and B Coy to LOEUILLY. C & D Coys as per programme.	
"	20.		Batt. transport less 2 limbers per Coy moved off to PAS area. "C" Coy moved from ST. FUSCIEN to CREUSE	
"	21.		Companies moved from CONTY AREA to PAS AREA. "A" Coy entrained at SALEUX 6 a.m. for DOULLENS arriving 10.40 a.m. marched to CORBIE reaching camp at 6 p.m. B Coy entrained SALEUX detrained DOULLENS. Embussed for MONDICOURT arriving 6.30 a.m. MAP. 57. N.E.	
			R.2.". "C" Coy left SALEUX at 11.35 a.m. various DOULLENS thence proceeding to TERRAMESNIL. D Coy r Bn. H.Q.	
			bivouced at PROUZEL and arrived at PAS at 6 a.m. on 22nd after detraining at MONDICOURT.	
PAS AREA	22.		Coys resting	
	23.		R.E. Coys in line. B Coy taking over the right sector with 13 guns. C Coy in Reserve 8 guns at FONQUEVILLERS 1 8 guns	
			at SOUASTRE. CASUALTIES NIL. A & D Coy preparing for the line.	Appendix V
RUCQUOY SECTOR	24.		A & D Coys carried off A line. A Coy taking over left sector with 16 guns & D Coy in support. CASUALTIES NIL.	
"	25.		VISIBILITY GOOD. Situation unchanged. Enemy Artillery Active. 6,000 rounds fired on F29a S.H. from F21C2&5.	
"	26.		VISIBILITY good. Artillery activity about normal. Hostile aircraft fairly active. 100 Rnd fired aimed from F29a	
			A Coy M.Gs entrained at F20b.10.45 & F26a.81 on L9&H.0 and L&H.6. Made new Positions at E 2.5 d 7099.	
			B Coy fired 7000 rounds F26a.10.45 & F26a.81 on L9&H.0 and L&H.6. made new Positions at E 2.5 d 7099.	
			C Coy & D Coy in Reserve & Support respectively. Batt Q in CHATEAU HENU.	
			Transport lines HENU. D. I. Q. C.	

Army Form C. 2118.

WAR DIARY
or
INTELLIGENCE SUMMARY.   June 1918

(Erase heading not required.)

Instructions regarding War Diaries and Intelligence Summaries are contained in F.S. Regs., Part II. and the Staff Manual respectively. Title pages will be prepared in manuscript.

Place	Date	Hour	Summary of Events and Information	Remarks and references to Appendices
BUCQUOY SECTOR	27		Enemy Artillery reported more active during last 24 hours. Aerial Activity also pronounced. Visibility good.	
			A Coy fired 14,500 rounds at following targets F23d.4.7. Rly Railway F29c.4. L46.00.35 - L56.00.35 F23d 90.30 - F23d 80.20 F23a 4.6.	
			B Coy fired 13,500 rounds at L9a.H.O. L4C 1.2. L8d.7.6 - L9C 80. L4d Sunken Rd. L4.6.54 and 300 rounds at E.A.	
			C Coy in support in Purfleet System and D Coy in Reserve.	
"	28		Enemy Artillery fairly active. Some aerial activity today. Visibility high. All day work no aerial carried out in time.	
			B Coy fired 9000 rounds on F23d 1370. X Roads F23d 4.6. Post F29c 1.4. Track F29c 9.1 -- F30 a 4.2.	
			C Coy fired 6000 Rounds on L9a 9.3. L66 65 Sunken Road L106. Bucks L106.30 - L4d 9.4.	
			D Coy in support and C Coy in Reserve.	
"	29		Enemy Artillery more active today. Aerial Activity less pronounced. Visibility Good.	
			A Coy fired 13,000 rounds on Railway F29c.d. Road F29c 1060. F29C 1.3 - F29C 1.5 F29a 65.35. battery on emplacements	
			B Coy fired 3000 rounds on L4C 13/8. Trench L4d 0525. L106920 Road L106 03 - L11 C O4.	
			C Coy in support and from F 25C 67 fired from 3-15-5.30 on Aubin of Activity L8a - L9C L8d - L9C 2000 rounds fired	
			C Coy in Reserve.	
			Casualties 2 O.R. wounded Shell. "D" Coy.	
	30		At night guns as distributed 6 guns being withdrawn & line rear of HENU.	Appendices VI
			Artillery Activity Considerably more. Activity in air fairly great. Visibility Good - important by evening	
			A Coy fired 4000 rounds at F29c 1/2 - 1.5 F29a 65.35 X Roads F23d 6.7. Track F29 a.A. L0.7 300 Rds at E.A.	

Army Form C. 2118.

WAR DIARY
or
INTELLIGENCE SUMMARY. JUNE 1918

(Erase heading not required.)

Instructions regarding War Diaries and Intelligence Summaries are contained in F. S. Regs., Part II. and the Staff Manual respectively. Title pages will be prepared in manuscript.

Place	Date	Hour	Summary of Events and Information	Remarks and references to Appendices
BUCQUOY	31.		A Coy from 4.00 10.a.a.t following. L80.2.7. L90 & L15.b. F29.a.t. L40.d and 750 at E.A.	
SECTOR			A Coy fired 2000 rds by day at L90.a.8.8. FORK L8c. Rouch L80.5.5 to L8c.1.3.	
			C coy in Reserve. Casualties NIL.	
			Movement of Officers. Arrivals. Departures.	
			Lt. BOOTH. E. 1.6.18 LT JUST J.C. Sick 19/6/18	
			Lt. LOWE T.C. 3.6.18	
			W TIMPERLEY T.L. 8.6.18	
			2/Lt PRIOR V.J. 12.6.18	
			2/Lt ROWE W. 12.6.18	
			2/Lt BLOOM J. 29.6.18.	
			The following OR's joined during month.	
			1 O.R. 3/6/18. 1 OR. 16/6/18	
			9 O.R's 10/6/18 1 OR 17/6/18.	
			34 OR's 12/6/18. 20 R's 27/6/18.	
			13 OR's 13/6/18	

SECRET.   COPY NO. 10.

37th Battalion, Machine Gun Corps.

Operation Order No. 33.

31st May 1918.

1. The following changes in the disposition of the 37th Bn. Machine Gun Corps will take place on Saturday morning 1st June.
"A" Coy. will move from ORVILLE to the BOIS DU WARNIMONT and take over the duties of "D" Coy.
"B" Coy. will move to ORVILLE for the purposes of training and field firing.

2. O.C. "D" Coy. will leave an Officer who will hand over and explain to O.C. "A" Coy. all duties regarding defence, counter-attack schemes, etc. This Officer will be attached to "A" Coy. until the night 1/2nd June for the purpose of showing disposition of M.Gs. etc. in the sector taken over.
O.C. "D" Coy. will leave 3 guides for the gun positions for the same period.

3. The responsibility regarding M.G. attachment to G.O.C. 63rd Inf. Bde. passes from O.C. "D" Coy. to O.C. "A" Coy. at 10 a.m. on 1st prox.

4. O.C. "A" Coy. will report at 63rd Inf. Bde. H.Q. as early as possible after taking over.

5. Both Companies will move at 10 a.m. and each will take over the accommodation vacated by the other. Small advanced parties will be sent the previous evening to take over.

6. Acknowledge (M.G. only).

Issued at Noon.

                                        Capt.
                        Adjt. 37th Bn. Machine Gun Corps.

COPIES TO:-
1. 37th Div. "G".
2. 63rd Inf. Bde.
3. Commanding Officer.
4. "A" Company.
5. "B" Coy.
6. "C" Coy.
7. "D" Coy.
8. Quartermaster.
9. Transport Officer.
10.) War Diary.
11.)
12. File.

SECRET.   Appendix II

37th Battalion, Machine Gun Corps   Copy No. 14
            Order No. 34.   6th June 1918.

Ref. Map AMIENS 17.
         1/100,000.

1. The following moves will take place tomorrow morning 7th June.
   (a) 'C' Coy 37 Bn. M.G. Corps will move to SEUX and take over the billets at present occupied by 'B' Coy in 112th Inf. Bde Area.
   (b) 'B' Coy will move to SAVEUSE and take over the billets occupied at present by 'C' Coy in the 111th Inf. Bde Area.
   (c) 'D' Coy will move to FOURDRINOY and occupy billets which will be allotted to them by Battn H.Qrs.

2. The completion of these moves will be reported to Battn. H.Qrs by 12 noon tomorrow.

3. In the event of a tactical move being ordered Companies will be attached to Brigades as under:
   'A' Coy will be attached to 63rd Bde (H.Qrs PICQUIGNY)
   'B' "   "   "   "   " 111th " (H.Qrs BOVELLES)
   'C' "   "   "   "   " 112th " (H.Qrs OISSY)
   'D' "   "   "   in Divisional Reserve.

4. Refilling. Rations for consumption on the 8th inst. will be drawn as already arranged, but 'B' Coy will arrange to hand over their rations to 'C' Coy at SEUX & 'C' Coy to hand over theirs to 'B' Coy at SAVEUX.
   'D' Coy will arrange for a guide to be left to bring their rations to FOUDRINOY.

Issued at 9.0 p.m.
                                    R.H. Peacock Capt.
                                  Adjutant 37th Bn, M.G. Corps

Copies to:
1. 37th Div G.   11. O/C 37th Div'l Train.
2.   "   " Q.   12. Transport Officer
3. 63rd Inf. Bde.   13. Quartermaster.
4. 111th Inf. Bde.   14/15 War Diary
5. 112th Inf. Bde.   16. File.
6. Commanding Officer
7. 'A' Coy 37th Bn M.G.Corps
8. 'B' "   "   "   "   "
9. 'C' "   "   "   "   "
10. 'D' "   "   "   "   "

Secret.   37th Battalion M.G. Corps   16

Operation Order No. 35   Appendix III

Ref: 1/100,000.
Amiens 17.

1. Division moves to an area E. of CONTY by bus and March Route today.

2. "A", "B" & "C" M.G. Coys will move under orders of the Infantry Brigade Groups to which they are attached.
H.Q. & "D" Coy. moves with the 112th Inf. Bde. Group.
Embussing point cross roads 400 yards S. of SAISSEVAL Church - BRIQUEMESNIL Road head at cross roads.
Embussing commences at 10.0 a.m.

3. Transport will move in accordance with orders from Group Commanders.
H.Q. & "D" Coy Transport will move with the troops of the 112th Inf. Bde. Group. Starting point cross roads 500 yards N.E. of QUEVAUVILLERS Church.
Head of 112th Inf. Bde. Group passes Starting Point at 11.15 a.m.

R.H. Seacock
Capt. & Adjt.
37th Battn. M.G. Corps.

10th June 1918.

Secret. 37th Bn Machine Gun Corps   Appendix V
                                              Copy No 16
               Order No 38
                                              22nd June 1918
Ref. Map 1/40000 Sheet 57D

1. The 37th Division will relieve the 62nd Division on the left Sector of the IV Corps Front on the nights of the 24/25th & 25/26th June 1918.

2. The 37th Bn M.G. Corps will relieve the 62nd Bn M.G. Corps as follows:—
   (a) On the afternoon of the 23rd June
       C Company 37th Bn will relieve B Coy 62nd Bn
       (8 guns in FONQUEVILLERS area and 8 guns SOUASTRE – Coy HQ D.22.a.1.9.
   (b) On the night 23/24th June
       B Coy 37th Bn will relieve D Coy 62nd Bn in Right Subsector. Relief to arrive at Coy HQ 10 pm
   (c) On the night 24/25th June
       A Coy 37th Bn will relieve A Coy 62nd in left Sector. Coy HQ F.B.C.7.1.
   (d) D Coy 37th Bn will relieve C Coy 62nd Bn in PURPLE LINE
       Note. Coy HQ are as they were previously unless otherwise stated.

3. All Company Commanders will meet Coy Commanders they relieve at 10 am tomorrow 23rd inst.

4. Belts specially packed in S.A.A. boxes will not be exchanged for ammunition. Belts in belt boxes may be exchanged under arrangement to be made by Coy Commanders. A certain number of belts in the area will be taken over as trench stores. No tripods will be exchanged.

5. 2 Officers and 72 other ranks of the Staff guides in the sector are attached for instruction. Coy Commanders will ascertain from their Officers how many there are in their Coys and will reduce their teams accordingly.
                                              (Over)

the numbers in each Group will at once be reported to the Quartermaster.

6. Trench aid area stores, maps, Defence schemes etc. will be taken over and copies of receipts sent to Bn HQ by 9 pm 26th inst.

7. Battalion H.Q. will close at PAS and be opened at HENU at an hour to be notified later

8. Our lorries will be at TERRAMESNIL at 2 pm tomorrow (23rd inst.) to take the teams of C Coy. which are going into the line, to SOUASTRE

9. Relief complete will be wired to Bn HQ by the code word "SWANAGE"

10. ACKNOWLEDGE (MG Bn Coys. only)

Issued at 9 pm

S.H. Peacock, Captain
Adjt 37th Bn M.G. Corps

Copies to:-
1. 37th Div. G
2.   "   Q.
3. County Officer
4. A Coy
5. B
6. C
7. D
8. 62nd MG Bn
9. 63rd Inf. Bde

10. 111th Inf. Bde
11. 112th
12. QM
13. BTO
14. Sig. Off
15. CMGO
16/1 War Diary
18/9 File

Appendix IV

Copy No. 10

37th Bath. H.Q. Corps.
Operation Order No. 36

Reg. Map.
AMIENS D.

1. "B" Coy. will move from FLEURY to NEUVILLE
SOUS-LOEUILLY this evening and take
over the responsibilities now carried by
93 Field Coy. R.E.
Move to be completed by 8 p.m.

2.

3. Confirmation of above to be reported to
Bn. H.Q.

Hours at 2.40 p.m.

Copy No. 1 — 37th Bat. G.
2. — do — G.
3. — do — adm.
4. "A" Coy.
5. "B" Coy.
6. "C" Coy.

7. "D" Coy.
8. M.G.
9. M.O.
10,11. Coys. Diary
12. File

Stracock
Capt. 37th Batt. M.G.

F.A. 74.

#1 Announcements: All Members to
37th Bn. M.G. Corps Order N° 38
                                    29th June 196
1. Parade for 1 hr. 26th inst. as at 9hrs 25 inst.
2. Paris 1st Battalion HQ on 26th close of PAS on
   12 noon 28th inst. and open at HENU at the
   same hour.

                    B. Shewick
                    Captain
                    Adjt 37th Bn. M.G. Corps.

Bolain Roads adjoining grades N° 38.

16   Secret   Appendix VI
                                              M.G. 121.

"A" Coy.   63rd Inf. Bde.   )
"B" "   2nd Bn. M.G.C.   ) For inf.
"C" "   "3" 37th Divn.   )
"D" "

──

    The following alterations in Machine Gun dispositions will take place on the night June 29/30th.

A. Left Group.
    Guns duplicated by guns of 2nd Division will be withdrawn as follows:-
        2 guns at F.14.d.4.1.
        2   "   " F.14.d.8.5.
        2   "   " F.15.c.5.9.

    Four of the above guns will be used to form a strong point at F.20.a.8.7. Until this is completed the teams will live in trenches in the neighbourhood away from the gun positions. Camouflage must be procured before work commences.

    The remaining 2 guns will relieve 2 guns of the purple group, at F.15.c.6.8.

B. Purple Group.
    The 2 guns duplicated by guns of the 2nd Division at F.15.c.7.1 will be withdrawn.

    4 guns of "D" Coy. will relieve 4 guns of "C" Coy. in the FONQUEVILLERS defences, and will be attached to "C" Coy. till further orders.

FONQUEVILLERS Group:-
4 guns of "C" Coy. will be withdrawn into reserve at HEBU.

All trench stores and S.A.A. will be removed from the abandoned emplacements. The positions will be pointed out to the Officer Commanding 2nd Battn. M.G. Co. so that they can be used as alternatives.

                                    L.A. Peacock, Captain,
                            Adjt. 37th Battn. Machine Gun Corps.
28.6.18.

37th Bn Machine Gun Corps

War Diary for the month of

July 1918

Army Form C. 2118.

WAR DIARY
INTELLIGENCE SUMMARY.
(Erase heading not required.) JULY 1918

Instructions regarding War Diaries and Intelligence Summaries are contained in F. S. Regs., Part II. and the Staff Manual respectively. Title pages will be prepared in manuscript.

Place	Date	Hour	Summary of Events and Information	Remarks and references to Appendices
BUCQUOY SECTOR			Artillery activity of enemy slightly less. Normal activity normal. Visibility good. Gun as detailed in O.O. 35 were changed	Ref. 1/10000 FRANCE Sheet 57 D.N.E.
	1		During the evening A Coy did some firing because of an Infantry Relief. Casualties One man wounded.	See
			A Coy took positions near LQc Road Fork L10a. Crew L4.B Road L4.B. 500 Round were fired. Groups re-organised.	Appendix I.
			C Coy in Reserve at SOUASTRE and HENU. D Coy for 4 guns with A & W.R. D Reserve & firm at FONQUEVILLERS.	Appx.
	2		Acclimatisation to unstrength. Artillery & aerial activity being average. Visibility was good. Casualties Nil.	
			A Coy fired 1500 rounds at Aricraft and 1500 Rounds on F29a 6.8. D Coy in Support	
			B Coy fired 300 rounds at E.A. and 6000 Rounds near L10a. FORK WOOD. Area L9.c and L9.d 78 - L9.c 80. C Coy in Reserve.	Appy
	3		Quiet day in the line but towards evening Enemy artillery became active. Aerial activity was marked. At 12.50 enemy M G/A.	
			fire Cylinders were projected into ABLAINZEVELLE area and A Coy assisted by firing with 8 guns 4000 rounds on F23d 3500. 4800 on F29.6 × 4800	
			on F28.6. 1000 rounds were fired on S.A. B Coy fired by day 1000 rounds into Area L.06 - L 5a. and 4000 rounds in Sunken Road in L10a. Area.	
			in L4d. L9d 050. 1300 rounds were fired on S.A. D Coy with 8 guns in Support & C Coy in Reserve training. Casualties Nil.	Appy
	4		During night 4/5 C Coy with 16 guns relieved "A" Coy. D Coy fired the foregoing with C Coy as the fourth. Activities normal all day	See Appendices
			B Coy fired 2000 rounds on enemy by day on L 40 x 44 + 1500 rounds on Trench L4c 3030 - L4c 0015. Also fired 1500 on Fork wood & 2250x40	Q.
			on Light Railway L9 c. 1000 Rounds fired on E.A. A Coy in Support. Casualties 2 ORs (one unknown at duty). Amongst the night 5 Cylinders were	
			used to harass gas appliance from the line. assisting the Special R.E. Coy.	Appy
	5		Situation Normal. Double ridge less active than usual. Visibility very high and Enemy observation balloons very much in evidence.	

Army Form C. 2118.

WAR DIARY
of
INTELLIGENCE SUMMARY. July. 1916.
(Erase heading not required.)

Instructions regarding War Diaries and Intelligence Summaries are contained in F. S. Regs., Part II. and the Staff Manual respectively. Title pages will be prepared in manuscript.

Place	Date	Hour	Summary of Events and Information	Remarks and references to Appendices
			REF 1/10,000 FRANCE SHEET 57D N.E.	
BUCQUOY SECTOR	6		B. Coy fired from 3pm-5pm. at Gomiecourt Road & Trenches in L10d. 1500rds. y FORK WOOD Road L26 cd. 1500, 3000 rounds were fired by rifle L10a.6.5 - L10c.2.7 and L13 a.4.6. 150 rounds fired at E.A. 6 Coy fired by day 1500 rds on L5Ab, L4d.5.2 - L4d.9.0. Road F29.c, F24 a 5.3 - 4.300 rds. 250 rounds fired at E.A. D Coy in Support. "A" Coy in Reserve. Casualties. 1 O.R. gas. 2 O.R. accidental M.G. & Rifle.	6/P.W.J
BUCQUOY SECTOR	6		Activity normal. Heavy barrage put down by us outside BUCQUOY 8.7pm - 8.38pm. Visibility good. Aerial Activity normal.	6/P.W.J
"			M.G. fire 950 rds at E.A. and 9000 rounds on road. L4c rds. trenches L4c. 9.6. L5b. 2.7. L5b. 6.1. Case L9.b. - A Coy in Reserve. D in Support.	
"	7		Coy fired 5,500 rds at Road F29a.4.9. F29.D.1. F23d a.9.0.0. F23.d.4.5.6.0 - F29.c.O.9. 115912 Lightd. Murray D. Killed day shell.	
			Any fairly quiet. Usual Battle Shelling. Aerial Activity slight. B Coy fired on L4b + L52.16. Trenches L4c + 9.6. L9c. 35. L9c. 90. L10a 12.5.4.	
			9.30 fired rounds fired. 500 rounds at E.A. C Coy fired 6000 rds at F29B.9.9. F 27A 3.3 F24a 0.2. Shot. Road L52.12.5.6. F29c Road. 500 Rds EA	
	8		D Coy in Support. A in Reserve. Casualties Nil. Partins being dug in FONQUEVILLE Rs. Wiring Green	6/P.W.J
			Situation much the same. Hostile shelling very heavy on KITE & RUM TRENCHES in E 29. Aerial Activity slight. Casualties Nil.	
			Right Group. B Coy fired 8000 rounds on L4b + L5a. L4c. L100 B. L6d. 31 - L6d. 8.9 Ans. L9c. And 750 rounds at E.A.	
			Left Group "C" Coy fired 1500 rounds on L4b.65 - L5a.9935 Ans. F30a4. F30 C. F24c 00.85 - F29a 9.9.0. F23d.2.8 F233.25.uS - F29 30.93.	
			F23 C. 9.7. 500 rounds fired at S.Q. Wiring positions being done. "D" Coy "A" Coy working at FONQUEVILLERS.	
			D Coy are still in Support and "A" Coy in Reserve. One Cas. O.R.	6/P.W.J
	9		Situation unchanged. Normal hostile activity. Aerial Activity normal. Visibility fair. Casts. Casualties 9.3.	
			Right Group fired L9C.3.5. - L15a.9.6. L9C. L8d.18.89. L9C.88. D Coy 6 guns in Support.	
			Left Group fired Ans. F30 D. F29C 53. F23D.7.2 L5 B Central. A Coy in Reserve.	6/P.W.J

Army Form C. 2118.

WAR DIARY
or
INTELLIGENCE SUMMARY. July 1918
(Erase heading not required.)

Instructions regarding War Diaries and Intelligence Summaries are contained in F. S. Regs., Part II. and the Staff Manual respectively. Title pages will be prepared in manuscript.

Place	Date	Hour	Summary of Events and Information	Remarks and references to Appendices
BUCQUOY SECTOR	10		Day Quiet. Hostile Aircraft not much in evidence. Visibility Poor & Poor. Showery Weather. Casualties Nil. A Coy in Reserve. D in Support.	REF 1/20,000 Sheet 57d N.E.
			Right Group fired on L4C 4589. Roads L4C4 & L9A and L8d9.8. 3970 rounds fired. Right Group fired on F33d.9065. Tm.	
			Rod. SR. Road Track F29C.9052. + Battery L5.6 Central. 6500 rounds fired.	
"	11		Fairly quiet day on whole. Enemy more active during the night. Aerial Activity more pronounced. Hostile flying planes being over own lines between 4 & 7 p.m.	Appx
			Right Group fired 8000 rounds on L4.1.14 wood L9.6.15.20 + L9C.8590. 100 rounds fired at EA. Enemy blew up 10 boxes SAA 16.8EA from at L13.5.7	
			Alt. Group fired 5300 rounds at F23d. Road. T.M. L4.6 F29C.6.4. F23d.4335. + F23D.6.3. Alt. Recce 'D' Coy Support. D.O. Reinforced.	Appx
	12.		Quiet day. Artillery + Aircraft not so active. Visibility Fair. Right Group fired Visibility Fair. Right Group fired 5500 rounds on L4C central. L4a 3.0 - 35 10 L28.88 90 L9 Oam.	Appx
			Right Group fired 1000 rounds on Tracks F29C and F23d. Battery F29C.0555 and L4b.6597. An. recce 'D' Support Casualties Nil. night 13/14 T.Y.	Appx
	13.		Quiet day. Aerial Activity normal. Much bombing at night. Alarms lines by our planes. At 3.15 am. Y3.25 am. M.Gs and Trench Artillery fired for two minutes each time on S.O.S lines. Visibility Poor. Rey high 6 - 8 p.m. Casualties 1 man wounded. Right Group fired on S.O.S.	
			Lines 41.8520 + 7500 rds on L4C central L4C 4589 - 3030. and L9A 3290-6580. 400 Rounds were fired at E.A. Left Group fired on S.O.S.	Appx
			8700 Rds and 6810 rounds on + Road F23d. L4b.6599. 956 Central. Battery F29C 05.55.	
	14.		This day was quiet on the sector but Enemy Artillery was active at night. Enemy Aircraft were more in evidence than on morning	Lee
			of 15. at 3 am 3.20 & 3.50 Aero in L4C - L10a were fired on in conjunction with Brig. R.A. Casualties Nil. "A" Coy relieved "B" Coy in Right.	Appendix 3
			Arryile Sector. B taking over from A in Reserve. Relief complete 10 a.m. A Coy fired 3250 rds on Road L4c + L10a. C Coy fires 6350 rds on	Appx
			F23/D.5.3. and trench on Road from L4C - L10a facing troops L4C Y.10a.	

Army Form C. 2118.

WAR DIARY
INTELLIGENCE SUMMARY.
(Erase heading not required.) JULY

Instructions regarding War Diaries and Intelligence Summaries are contained in F. S. Regs., Part II. and the Staff Manual respectively. Title pages will be prepared in manuscript.

REF 1/20,000 FRANCE SHEET 57D N.E.

Place	Date	Hour	Summary of Events and Information	Remarks and references to Appendices
HQ 73			Day fairly quiet on our front. Burrows of N. NZ. reached Forres at 3.40 pm & 9.30 pm. Visibility Good. E.A. actively abght. Casualties Nil	
BUCQUOY SECTOR	15.		A Coy fired during night in conjunction with Artillery 3000 Rounds on Road 13d - L9b Track L9d. Road in L9a.76. C Coy fires 2,300 Rds on Track L9.B.	APPX
	16		L.9.B. Track in L.9a and Artillery & 4000 rounds on X Roads F.23d. Bdy in Reserve Bn to support	
			Day much more active Artillery & Aerial Activity increased Visibility Good. Mayfield 1200 Rds at aircraft 700 Rds at Road in L.4.T. C & D Trenches in L.4.C and at L.8.0.1.8.24. C Coy fired on L.4.B.6.4 L.5.a.99.40 F.23d. S.O.S. line F.9.6 at E.A. Bomb. Casualties Coy M.T. H.9.57 rounds	APPX
	17		Day fairly active. Visibility Good. Many Balloons up. Bdy fired 6500 rds on F.23d.9.0.8. F.29.6.8.2 F.29.D.1.a. L.5.a. 80.25. A Coy fired 6500 rds on Trench & Rd L.4.B. Trench L.9.C. & Track in L.9.a. & at Enemy Aircraft. Casualties Nil.	APPX
	18		Enemy Artillery more active, but E.A. inactive. At 2 A.M. on night 18/19. The III Brigade raided an enemy post at F.28d. 90 credit 4 guns field Coy & 10 guns of C Coy cooperated in accordance with M.G. 2.25 attacks. 25000 rds being fired. 1000 Rds were fired on F.23D between 5 & 6 p.m. on centre of movement. B Coy Support. B Coy in Reserve. Casualties 1 O.R. wounded.	dee Appendix 4. APPX
	19		A lively day in this sector. Artillery active & aircraft on both sides particularly so Alaynight. E.S.S.A.R.T.S. probed by enemy S.O.S. sent up on our right. Enemy Balloon shot down. Q. Coy fired 5000 rds Road L.100.v.B. Road & Trench L.4.D. Trench in L.8.d. C Coy fired 3000 rds on Rd F.30.a. Track F.29.c. & Road L.4.D. No Casualties. 11 O.R's gone on Reinforcement May.	APPX
	20.		Enemy Artillery Quieter. N.Z. Burrows moving freGot forward on our right. For News reports taken by our troops Visibility Good. A Coy fired 3500 rds on L.9.25.84. Trenches L.4. and Q Coy fired 100 rds at E A. hinds of our Line not quite within insight. and 400 rds on Fn. B.65.SP F.29.C F.30.a. F.23.d Roads Casualties Nil. B Coy Reserve. D in Support	APPX

WAR DIARY or INTELLIGENCE SUMMARY

Army Form C. 2118.

JULY 1918

REF. 1/10,000 FRANCE SHEET 57°N.E

Place	Date	Hour	Summary of Events and Information	Remarks and references to Appendices
20/7/18 BUCQUOY SECTOR	21		Artillery somewhat quieter today, but aeroplanes very active. B Coy fired 75 rds on front in L.4.c. by day for instructional purposes. & 2000 rounds in trench L.1.0.6.a. C Coy fired 6000 rds on roads F.29.c. L.5.b. & F.29.b. B Coy Reserve. D's Suffolks	69/7
	22		An active day. Our Artillery very active and so were our own planes. At midnight Barrage on our left front and our left Group acc'd by firing 3000 rounds on area F.23.d while each gun in support fires 300 rounds were fired at intervals during night. 2000 rounds on F.29.b	69/7
			Lf. Group fired 4000 rds on Pimple Trench L.4.6. & L.c rd. 2000 on Huts L.4.c rd. 2000 rds direct on FORK WOOD and Pavemetain & 75 rds on L.4.C.7.9.	
			B Coy in Reserve. D Company in support. Visibility High. A Enemy balloons up all day.	69/7
	23		Fairly active day. Enemy took H.As. our posts in the morning North to the frontier. H Middleham raided enemy at night will discovered several prisoners in…	See Appendices
			Our Artillery Cos operated firing 2,3000 rounds according to programme 0.0.42. C Coy Lf.Group also fired 1,000 rds by day on L. & L.25. 3b.	5
			-65.20 and 1800 rds on E.29.c. and E.29.c. 90.55. Casualties 1 O.R. Killed & 1 wounded	69/7
	24		Fairly quiet day. Aid on our right advanced their posts S.A. fairly lively. Visibility Good. A Coy fired 6,150 Rds. on Sanders rds L.4.C. HQ. L.9.a. Trench & Trench L.9.c. H.Q. L.5.a.	
			A Coy fired 10000 rds on F.30.a. 15.55. F.29.6.ren. F.23.c. 04.12-5.2. CASUALTIES NIL	
			Lt.Col. W.H.C. PERRY-KNOX-GORE took over Command of this Battalion fr O.R. E.O. RASDEN. M.C. to England.	69/7
	25		Lively day. Germans attack by enemy on our Right. Cleaves Hf. Unsuccessful. A Coy fired 4070 rounds on L.1.0.6.rd. 14.a. Repair	
			trenches L.96. Trench L.4.C rd. our Road L.40. 90.3.8. C Coy fired on Road L.4.b. Barrage F.29 6 road n F.23.d. an't fire F.29.c.5730- F.29.c.005 Support 75	
			6000 rounds were fired. Casualties Nil. At night B Coy Relieves D Company in frontline, and also the guns of D Coy attached	See Appendices
			to the Right Lt. Group. Visibility to-day was fair to good.	69/7

Army Form C. 2118.

WAR DIARY
or
INTELLIGENCE SUMMARY.
(Erase heading not required.) JULY

Instructions regarding War Diaries and Intelligence Summaries are contained in F. S. Regs., Part II. and the Staff Manual respectively. Title pages will be prepared in manuscript.

Place	Date	Hour	Summary of Events and Information	Remarks and references to Appendices
BUCQUOY SECTOR.	26.		Quiet day. Very unsettled weather. Enemy aerial activity slight. A Coy fired 9000 rds on Cmds L4C Trench Tracks L4C 1520 – L4C 4058. L9C 1555-L.	REF 57D NE [initials]
		10.01.070	C Coy fired 6500 rds on L4b F23d 7.6 F29 55.25 Road L4b. H.Q. Coy. 9. OR wounded shell. B Support Coy. D Reserve Coy.	[initials]
	27		Weather very bad. Aerial activity Nil. At 1-15am when in L.B. was gassed by projector. Guns of right group completed relieved over until morning. Fired 11,900 rds on Trencks L8C L8d Road Tracks L8d L9a. Left Group fired 6000 on Road & Tracks L4b. South L5a 1-5, F29 c 10, X Rds F23d.	[initials] FRANCE
	28.		Quiet day. Visibility very good. Casualties Nil. A Coy fired 6100 Rds on Road L4c, Road L8d, Road L6, and Road in L100. C Coy fired 9500 Rds on Rd pts L465-3 and L5a 2.3. Tracks L9b - L10c. F24c 14.10 – 36.34 – 7000 Rds. Bty in Support. D in Reserve.	20,000 [initials]
	29.		Fairly active day. Visibility poor owing to haze. Alry fired 6080 rds on neighbourhood of FORK WOOD. L9A. Railway in L9C C. Coy fired 6000 Rds on F23d 5-7. F24 C0096. L4b 10-10 – 070. B Coy Reserve. D in Support. 1 OR Wounded Shell.	[initials]
	30.		Another quiet day. Active night. Barrage on our right heavily shelled 0.2.15 and night 30/31. 1st Pri. Sussex regiment raided enemy pests IN G.2. C Coy operates Rifle CB. H.A. A Coy she fired 35 barrages on Tracks L8d Road in L4b+C C Coy also fired on Rds F23d+F24C on tracks F9c Rd in L.b.C.	Appendix 1. [initials]
			B Coy in Support. A Coy in Reserve. Casualties NIL.	
	31.		Fairly active day with Artillery on both sides. Visibility very good. Hostile weather made aerial activity more pronounced. Casualties Nil. A Company fired 3000 rds on Wreua in L9C x 3000 on Road L9b. L4C 7.9 L4d 07. Blvy fired 5500 rds on F24 a Tracks F280 Tracks F29c 92.52 - F29d 13.10. L4C 70.78 – L4C 3032.	[initials]

WAR DIARY
or
INTELLIGENCE SUMMARY.

(Erase heading not required.) July

Army Form C. 2118.

Place	Date	Hour	Summary of Events and Information	Remarks and references to Appendices
			The following changes took place during the month.	
			1) Lieut. W.H. le Page-Roeth gave Junior Maid 20.27/4/18 and to took over command on 24/7/18 from Lt. Col. Bastow M.C.	
			2) Col. P.D. Bastow M.C. departed for England 23/1/7/18.	
			3) Medical attached for duty 30/7/18 as T.O. on probation	
			1) Pte. Arment. Transferred to 37' Signal Coy. R.E. 3.7.18	
			2) Cpl. Sergent. Transferred to IV Army Sig. Coy. 6.7.18	
			3) S.S.M. Dumpleby. to Hospital 11.7.18	
			4) Pte. Hall. do 10.7.18	
			5) O/M. M.C. Granville do 17.7.18	
				Animal Casualties
				2 Mules Killed
				Gassed 14/7/18. Evac 25/7/18
				Wounded & Evacuated.
				Evac 14-7-18
			The following Reinforcements joined during the month.	Wounded & remaining
			July 1. Two O.Rs. July 12. One O.R. July 28. 11 O.Rs.	on lines.
			July 2. Three O.Rs. July 16. One O.R. July 29. 4 ORs Three ORs	
			July 4. One O.R. July 20. Eleven O.Rs.	Two. 23.7.
			July 9. One O.R. July 23. Three O.Rs.	

Hy. Page le Pel. Lieut-Col.

Commanding 37th Bn. Machine Gun. Corps.

SECRET.   Appendix 1
Copy No. 10

37th BATTALION. MACHINE GUN CORPS.

Order No. 39   1st July 1918.

1. The following changes in dispositions will take place on the night 1st/2nd July.
   (a) Two guns of "A" Coy. in F.22.central will relieve 2 guns of "B" Coy. in F.27.a.
   The guns relieved in F.27.a. will relieve 2 guns of "D" Coy. at E.30.a.
   The guns relieved at E.30.a. will relieve the remaining 2 guns of "C" Coy. in the FONQUEVILLERS Group, which will return to HENU.
   (b) An inter-relief will take place between the 2 guns of "D" Coy. in F.25.a. and the 2 guns of "B" Coy. in F.26.b, to enable the latter to be included in the Southern Brigade Group and the former in the Northern Brigade Group.

2. Details of relief to be arranged between Company Commanders concerned.

3. On completion of relief, O.C. "A" Coy. will assume command of the 20 guns in the Northern Brigade Group, O.C. "B" Coy. the 20 guns in the Southern Brigade Group, and O.C. "D" Coy. the FONQUEVILLERS Group.

4. After relief, dispositions will be as follows:-

__Northern Brigade Group.__

2 guns	F.21.b.	4 guns	F.20.a.
2 "	F.21.c.	2 "	F.19.c.
4 "	F.21.d.	2 "	E.24.b.
2 "	F.27.a.		
2 "	F.26.b.		

__Southern Brigade Group.__

4 guns	F.26.a.	2 guns	E.23.d.
4 "	F.25.d.	2 "	L.1.b.
2 "	F.25.a.	2 "	L.1.d.
2 "	F.30.a.		
2 "	F.24.c.		

__FONQUEVILLERS Group.__

1 gun	E.16.d.	2 guns	E.28.a.
2 guns	E.22.d.	2 "	E.27.b.
1 gun	E.22.b.		

5. M.G.Coys. acknowledge by wire.

Issued 12 noon.

R.Seacock Captain,
Adjt. 37th Bn. Machine Gun Corps.

Copies to:-
1. "A" Coy.   5. 37th Division "G".   9/10. War Diary.
2. "B" "   6. 63rd Inf. Bde.   11/12. File.
3. "C" "   7. 111th Inf. Bde.
4. "D" "   8. ~~XXXXXXXXXXXX~~
              2nd Bn. M.G.C.

SECRET.   Copy No. 14

37th Battalion. Machine Gun Corps.

Operation Order No. 40.   2nd July 1918.

1. The following changes will take place in the dispositions of 37th Battalion, Machine Gun Corps.
 "C" Coy. will relieve "A" Coy. in the Northern Brigade Group of the Left Division Sector on the night 3rd/4th July.

2. The four guns of "D" Coy. attached to "A" Coy. will remain in position and will come under orders of O.C. "C" Coy. on completion of relief.

3. All details of relief will be arranged between Company Commanders concerned.

4. All defence schemes, maps, S.O.S. lines, and trench stores will be handed over and receipts obtained. Details of work under construction, and other work proposed will also be handed over.

5. On completion of relief "A" Coy. will take over the accommodation vacated by "C" Coy.

6. Relief complete will be wired to this office by code word BOXER.

7. Acknowledge. (M.G.Coys. only).

Issued at 9 p.m.

S.H. Peacock Captain,
Adjt. 37th Battn. Machine Gun Corps.

Distribution:-
Copies to:-
1. 37th Division. "G".
2. 63rd Infantry Brigade.
3. 112th   "   "
4. Commanding Officer.
5. Maj.J.G.P.Rideal D.S.O.
6. "A" Coy.
7. "B" Coy.
8. "C" Coy.
9. "D" Coy.
10. Quartermaster.
11. M.T.O.
12. Signalling Officer.
13. 37th Div.Sig.Coy.R.E.
14/1. War Diary.
15/17. File.

Above relief hurriedly postponed owing to in projector attack.
Copy of letter to O.C A & C Coys sent by Special D.R.
Secret & very urgent.
R/S. 27.   3rd July.
Reference this office O.O. 40 matter therein referred to will not take place tonight. Same times and places will hold good for tomorrow.
(Sgd) John G P Rideal Major
for Lieut.-Col.
Commanding 37th Bn. Machine Gun. Corps.

Bn Head Qs.

Identification Trace for use with Artillery Maps.

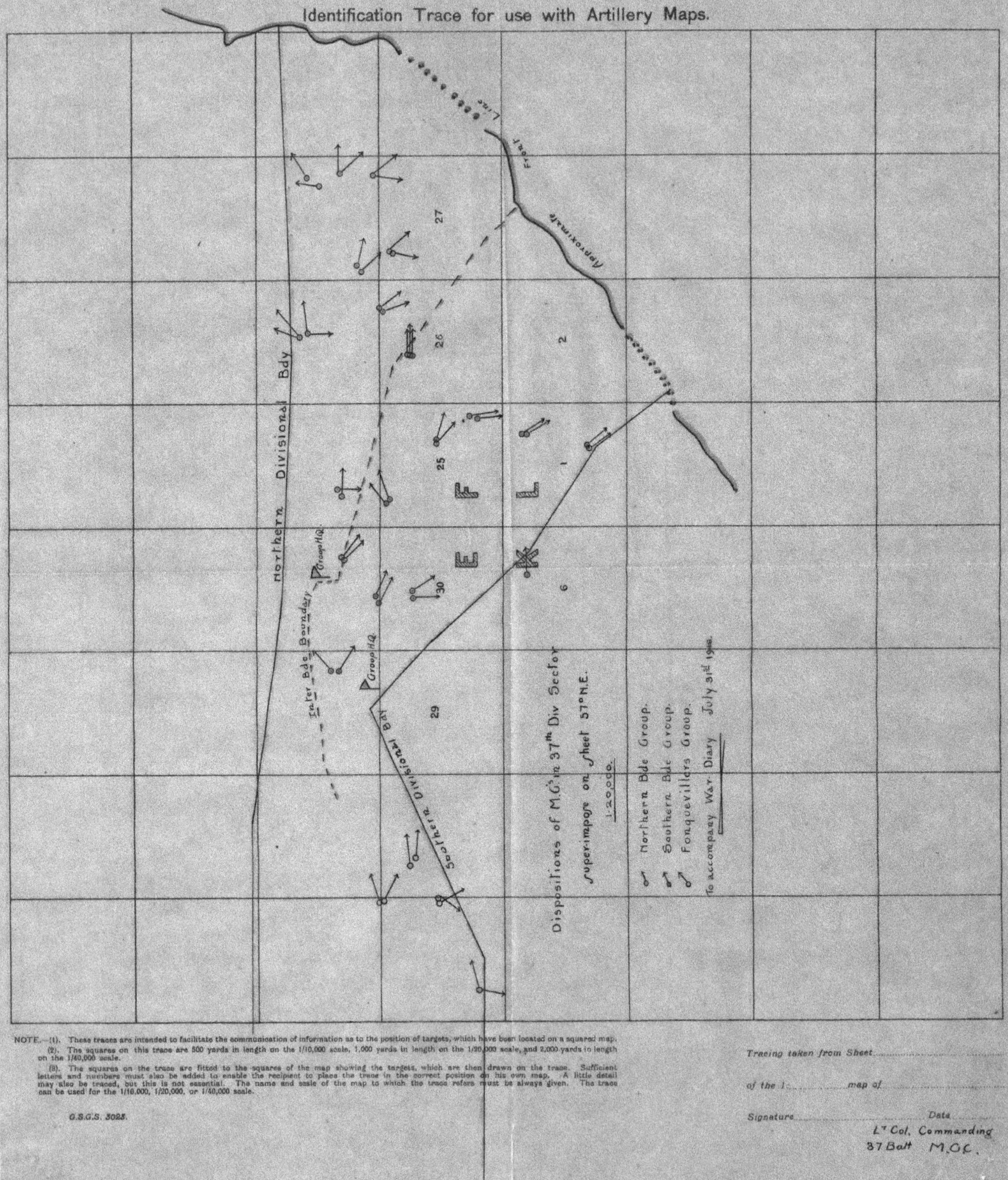

Northern Divisional Bdy
Inter Bde Boundary
Southern Divisional Bdy
Front Line
Hebuterne

Group HQ
Group HQ
Group HQ

27
26
2
25
E F L L
30
6
29

Dispositions of M.G's in 37th Div Sector
Superimposed on Sheet 57^dN.E.
1:20,000.

o— Northern Bde Group.
↗ Southern Bde Group.
o— Fonquevillers Group.

To accompany War Diary July 3rd 1916.

NOTE.—(1). These traces are intended to facilitate the communication of information as to the position of targets, which have been located on a squared map.
(2). The squares on this trace are 500 yards in length on the 1/10,000 scale, 1,000 yards in length on the 1/20,000 scale, and 2,000 yards in length on the 1/40,000 scale.
(3). The squares on the trace are fitted to the squares of the map showing the targets, which are then drawn on the trace. Sufficient letters and numbers must also be added to enable the recipient to place the trace in the correct position on his own map. A little detail may also be traced, but this is not essential. The name and scale of the map to which the trace refers must be always given. The trace can be used for the 1/10,000, 1/20,000, or 1/40,000 scale.

G.S.G.S. 3025.

Tracing taken from Sheet _____
of the 1: _____ map of _____
Signature _____ Date _____
Lt Col. Commanding
37 Batt M.G.C.

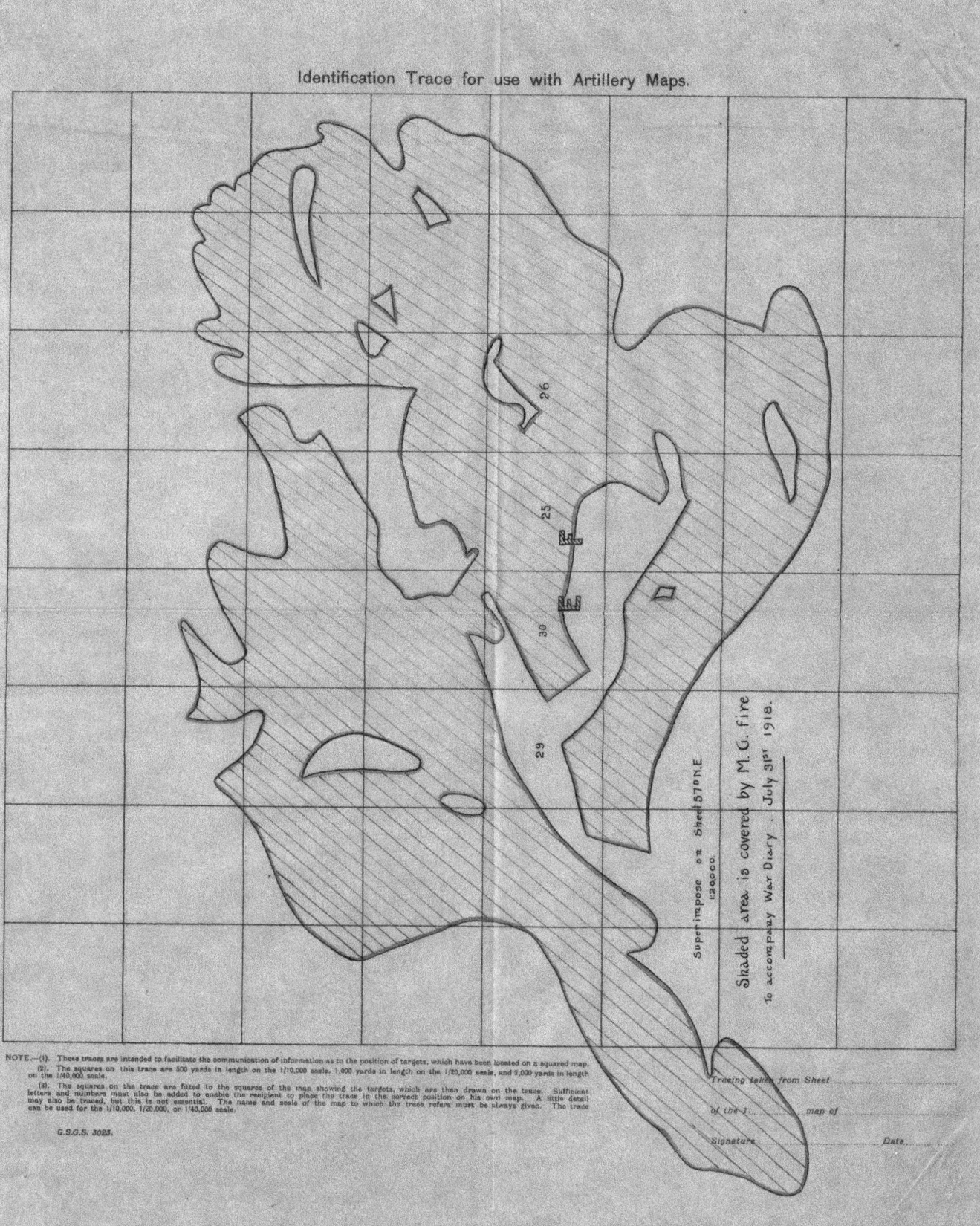

Appendix 3.

SECRET.   37th Battalion, Machine Gun Corps.   Copy No. 7

Operation Order No. 41.

                                                         11th July 1918.
Ref. Map.
Sheet 57.D. N.E. 1/20,000.

1. "A" Company, 37th Battalion, Machine Gun Corps, will relieve
   "B" Company, in the Southern Brigade Group on the night of
   the 14th/15th July.

2. Details of relief will be arranged between Company Commanders
   concerned.

3. On completion of the relief, O.C. "A" Company will take
   over the command of the twenty guns of the Southern Brigade
   Group.

4. After relief, "B" Company will take over the present accommodation and duties of "A" Company.

5. Officers will reconnoitre the area beforehand, and one man
   per team of "A" Company will be attached to corresponding
   teams of "B" Company for twentyfour hours before relief.

6. All Maps, Defence Schemes, Trench Stores, Work proposed and
   in hand, will be carefully handed over, and copies of
   Receipts sent to this office within 24 hours of relief.

7. Completion of relief will be wired to this office by the
   code "BARNET".

8. Acknowledge. (M.G. Corps only)

           Issued at 6.0 p.m.

                                      R H Peacock
                                              Captain,
                      Adjutant, 37th Battn. Machine Gun Corps.

Copies to:-

1. 37th Division. "G".   8. "C" Company.
2. 63rd Infantry Brigade.   9. "D"   "
3. 111th   "   "   10. Quartermaster.
4. 112th   "   "   11. Bn. Transport Officer.
5. U.S. M.G. Battalion.   12. Bn. File.
6. "A" Company.   13. War Diary.
7. "B"   "

    12 37th Sq. C.
     B Bn. S.O.

appendix 4

SECRET.

"C" Coy. 37th B'n.M.G.C.
"A" " do do

"Q" 37th Division.) For information.
111th Inf. Bde.)

1. The 111th Brigade are raiding the enemy post at   S.A.A. total.
   F.28.d.0.0. at a time and date which has been
   notified to Coy. Commanders.

2. Machine Guns will co-operate as follows:-

   "A" Coy. 4 guns will be moved forward to about
   L.3.3.9.5. and will engage the road from L.4.a.2.5.
   to L.4.b.3.5. Fire will commence at Zero and will
   cease at Zero plus 20. Rate of fire 125 rounds
   per gun per minute.   10,000

   "C" Coy. 4 guns at F.21.b.5.1.will engage area
   F.22.d.8.2. - L.3.a.2.8. - F.29.c.8.1. - F.28.d.9.5.
   with intermittent bursts from Zero minus 90 to Zero.   4,000
   and at the rate of 75 rounds per gun per minute
   from Zero - Zero plus 20.   6,000

   2 guns at F.26.b.5.8. will search the trench
   system at F.29.a.9.5. from Zero to Zero plus 20
   minutes. Rate of fire 75 rounds per gun per minute.   3,000

                                                                23,000

3. Officers of "A" and "C" Coys will synchronise watches
   and confirm the hour of Zero at Headquarters 111th Brigade
   at 6.p.m.to-night.

4. Acknowledge. (M.G.C.units only).

                                       R.Heacock Capt & Adjt
                                       for   Lieut-Col.
18/7/18.   Commanding 37th B'n.Machine Gun Corps.

Appendix 5

SECRET.

COPY NO. 10
July 22nd/18.

37TH BATTALION MACHINE GUN CORPS.

OPERATION ORDER NO. 42.

Total S.A.A.
expenditure.

1. A raid will be carried out on the night Zero/24th inst by the 63rd Infantry Brigade on the enemy's trenches running from L.2.d.30.90. to L.2.a.71.01.

2. Machine Guns will co-operate as follows:-

   (a) Arrangements have been made with the New Zealand Division for 2 guns of "A" Coy. to move to about L.7.a.8.7. to bring on L.8.b.3.0. - L.8.b.8.8.

   Time. Zero to Zero plus 7 minutes, 200 rounds per gun
                                                    per minute.   2,800

   These guns will be laid direct in daylight.

   (b) 4 guns of "A" Coy. will move to about L.2.a.8.8. to cover the area L.8.d.

   Time. Zero to Zero plus 15 minutes, 150 rounds per gun)
                                                    per minute.)
         Zero plus 15 to Zero plus 25, 80 rounds per gun) 12,600
                                                    per minute.)

   (c) 4 guns of "C" Coy. will move to about F.27.a.5.1. and will cover the area L.9.b. particularly the trench running North and South.

   Time. Zero to Zero plus 15 minutes, 150 rounds per gun)
                                                    per minute.) 12,600
         Zero plus 15 to Zero plus 25, 80 rounds per gun)
                                                    per minute.)
                                                                    _____
                                                                     28,000

3. Zero hour and arrangements for synchronisation of watches will be notified later.

4. Acknowledge. (M.G.C. Units only).

Issued at 11-30. a.m.

J Thomason Lt/Col
                                                                    Capt. &
                                                    Adjt. 37th B'n. Machine Gun Corps.

COPIES TO:-
   1. 37th Div. "G".   6. "D" Coy.
   2. 63rd Inf. Bde.   7. Sig. Officer.
   3. "A" Coy.   8. N.Z. M.G.B'n.
   4. "B" "   9. File.
   5. "C" "   ✓10/11. War Diary.

Appendix 6

SECRET.   COPY NO. 11

REF. MAP.   37TH BATT" MACHINE GUN CORPS.   July 23rd/18.
57.D.N.E. 1/20,000.
                              OPERATION ORDER NO. 43.

1. "B" Coy. 37th B'n. M.G. Corps will relieve "D" Coy. 37th B'n. M.G.
    Corps ~~Bn~~ on the night 25th/26th, as follows:-

    (a) One section will relieve the section of "D" Coy. at present
        attached to "C" Coy. in the Northern Brigade Group.

    (b) One section will relieve the section of "D" Coy. at present
        attached to "A" Coy. in the Southern Brigade Group.

    (c) Two sections and H.Q. will relieve the two sections and H.Q.
        of "D" Coy. in the FONQUEVILLERS Group.

2. Advance parties consisting of O.C. "B" Coy, 1 N.C.O. per section,
    and 1 O.R. per gun team will be attached to "D" Coy. for 24 hours
    prior to relief.

3. Details of relief will be arranged by Coy. Commanders concerned.

4. On relief "D" Coy. will take over the present duties and accomo-
    dation of "B" Coy.

5. All programmes of work, defence schemes, trench and area stores
    etc. will be taken over and copies of receipts forwarded to this
    Office within 24 hours of relief.

6. Completion of relief will be notified by wiring the code word
    "GARNET".

7. Acknowledge. (M.G. Units only).

    Issued at 12. noon.

                                                    R.H. Peacock
                                                                        Capt. &.
                                                    Adjt. 37th B'n. Machine Gun Corps.

    COPIES TO:-
                1. 37th Div. "G".   7. Quartermaster.
                2. "A" Coy.   8. O.C. Signal Coy.
                3. "B" "   9. 9th N. Staffs.
                4. "C" "   10. File.
                5. "D" "   11/12. War Diary.
                6. Sig. Officer.

.SECRET.

Copy No. 10

Appendix ?

37th BATTALION. MACHINE GUN CORPS.

Operation Order No. 44.

29th July 1918.

Ref. Map.
Sheet 57 D.N.E. FRANCE. 1/20,000.

1. A raid will be carried out by the 1st Battalion The Essex Regt. on a date and at a time to be notified later, against the following objectives.

    First objective. Outpost line. F.28.d.70.70. to F.29.a.00.25.
    Second objective. Main line. F.29.c.00.90. to F.29.a.30.20.

2. Machine Guns of 37th Battalion, M.G.Corps. will co-operate as follows:-

No. of Guns.	Targets.	No. of Rds.	Remarks.
Right Brigade Group.			
2.	Trenches, Rd. & Posts near Crucifix L.4.a.	5400.	Search.
3.	Trenches N. & S. of Rd. in L.4.b.	8100.	
Left Brigade Group.			
4.	F.28.d.35.35.) F.28.d.55.05.) F.28.d.90.25.) F.29.c.05.45.)	10800.	Area Shoot.
2.	F.29.a.50.75.	5400.)	Traverse to cover left flank.
2.	F.29.a.75.50.	5400.)	
4.	Re-entrant trenches in F.29.b. & d.	10800.	

3. Rate of fire for all guns:-

    Zero to zero plus 7. 150 rds. per minute.
    Zero plus 7 to Zero plus 17. Intermittent bursts 75 rds. per minute.
    Zero plus 17 to Zero plus 22. 150 rds. per minute.
    Zero plus 22 to Zero plus 24. Intermittent bursts.

4. Details as to date, zero hour, and synchronisation will be notified later.

5. Acknowledge. (M.G.Units only)

    Issued at 5.30 p.m.

J. Thomson D. for
Captain,
Adjutant, 37th Battn. Machine Gun Corps.

P.T.O.

Copies to:-
1. 37th Division. "G".
2. 63rd Infantry Brigade.
3. 111th   "   "
4. 112th   "   "
5. "A" Company.
6. "B" Company.
7. "C"   "
8. File.
9. C.R.A.
10/11. War Diary.

37th Bn M.G.C. WAR DIARY

For month of August 1918.

Army Form C. 2118.

WAR DIARY
or
INTELLIGENCE SUMMARY.

(Erase heading not required.) *August*

Instructions regarding War Diaries and Intelligence Summaries are contained in F. S. Regs., Part II. and the Staff Manual respectively. Title pages will be prepared in manuscript.

Place	Date	Hour	Summary of Events and Information	Remarks and references to Appendices
			REF MAP 1/200000 FRANCE SHEET 57 N.E. & 1/40,000 FRANCE SHEET 57 D	
BUCQUOY SECTOR	1		Sector defended by 48 Machine Guns. – A right and A left group of 20 guns each forward and 8 guns in FONQUEVILLERS. One Company in Reserve with 8 guns M.H.Q. at SOUASTRE D.29.a.1.8. and 8 guns in Transport lines at HENU. D.19.c. Bn. Head Qrs. HENU C.24.b.8.9.	Posey Kenny
			Weather very fine. No enemy air activity on Ain. 1 in Octelbeg was apparent. A Coy fired 900 rds on Road L.H.C.M. Roads LgB. Tracks L.9.c. & L.14.a. 750 rds on new field gun E.A. C Coy fired 6500 Rds on works in F.29a. Tracks F.29 d. v. L.9.a. Casualties Nil.	Posey Kenny
	2		Fine to cloudy. Bn. front. Activity in Air. 1 enemy scout by upper alt. Heavy rain fell all day reducing the trenches bad. C Coy fired 5000 rds on aerial road. L.9 D.H.b. Trenches 9.L.C. – L.4.b. Track L.4.C.7.7 – L.9.C.B.3. C Coy fired 6000 rds on F.9.C.9.8. Road L.H.C.M. Tracks 74C. Bucn F.9.b. Casualties Nil.	Posey Kenny
	3		Mild weather conditions slightly improved. Artillery Posts actively increased. A Coy fire 8000 Rds on following tracks L9b. Area form'd at O.P. and L.14.B.20.98. C Coy fired 9000 rds on trew F29c. 5.3. L.9.O.4.4. F.9.a. 10.50. Track F.9.a.9.4 – F.9.b.2.3. Corps new fire safely on F.9.9. 15.00. Casualties Nil.	Posey Kenny
	4		Heavy gusts and Artillery. – Aircraft now active on both sides. On situation was constantly 18"K R.R.C. in cavalcade with 1/1 Coy fire 2.500rds on L.9.c. 5.3.87.	Posey Kenny
			8300 rds were fired also on FORK WOOD Trench L.4.C. C Coy fired 0.500 rds NW Bn F.130.15 B. F.23.d.8.8. F.9C. 5.65. L.9c.47. Casualties Nil.	
	5		Weather dull. Relief proceeded. Arcy 1st B Coy was relieved by D Coy pcds. O.D.1.15. Harassing fire in usual carried out. 3500 GCPO rds being fired on track trench L.9.a. Road L.4.D.1.50. Trew F.23.D.6.2 Tracks F.29.c.11. – F.9.C.14. Night Cy fire for tracks in L.9.6. and Thiepval-Arras in L.9.b. Casualties Nil.	
	6		15 Inch Arty began supplies to Fateque to Special Arty R.E.a. Fairly active day. Better weather conditions helpful aerial activity enemy planes scored across round E.29. A. Coy fired 6000 rounds on Area L.8d.e.6 – L.8.a.5.1. and from L.9.B.5 & L.14 central. B Coy did no firing. Fatigue carried supplies upto for 5" but were linked back. Enemy 8-enemy shelling. Casualties Nil.	Posey Kenny

WAR DIARY or INTELLIGENCE SUMMARY

Army Form C. 2118.

Place	Date	Hour	Summary of Events and Information	Remarks and references to Appendices
BUCQUOY SECTOR	7.		Activity normal. Prisoner of 11 Coy Reserve Bn. captured by 63 Bde. Bde. patrol this morning. In anticipation of hostile attack tonight Regt Group fired 23,000 Rds on vehicle areas from ABLAIN ZEVELLE to LOG EAST WOOD – BUCQUOY ROAD. Regtl. Group Rifle Strength "A" & "B" Coys. 4 Coys + Scouts Bundle on L.9.a. firing 7000 Rds. CASUALTIES 2 hynes Gas.	Left 77 ... Right Regt Group
"	8		Activity normal in own sector, but heavy bombardment heard to South. Visibility good. Aerial activity normal. "A" Coy fired 7000 Rds on L4 & L5A. L.8.D.25. L.8.a.99 – B.9: 750 at aircraft + 250 Rounds sniping. "B" Coy fired 9500 rds on Tracks F.9.C. L.5.A. F.23.b. – F.2.a. and F.3.a. Casualties Nil.	Map 1: 20,000 France Sheet 57 NE
"	9		Activity normal: 112th Inf. Bde. relieved 111th Inf. Bde. in right sector. Visibility good. Aerial activity normal. "D" Coy fired 5500 Rds on Road L4.c.y.d, L.0.b.58, L.9.c.b, Track L.4.c.22 to L4.c.5.6: 1000 at aircraft + 4470 Rds sniping. "B" Coy fired 7000 Rds on tracks in F.23.d + F.2.a.c. Tracks F.9.c. and Road in L4.b. Casualties Nil.	
"	10		Quiet day in the line. S.O.S. signal was sent up on left sector about L4.a. and was answered by our guns. Right Group firing 3750 rds at 3:18 a.m. and left Group 11000 rds: Harassing fire was also carried out "A" Coy firing 6000 rds on L.9.c.8. L.9.b.6. Road L4.c.d. Track junction L4.c.5.6, 1500 rds at aircraft. and "D" Coy firing 9000 rds on tracks F.9.c.20.60, Road L4.b, F.23.d.8 F.2.a.c.12.90, F.23.d.5.0 F.2.a.c.2.h. Visibility good. Aircraft more active. Casualties Nil. –	
"	11		Activity normal. Visibility good. Aerial activity normal. "A" Coy fired 5000 rds on Road and track L4.a.b, +c, L.9.b.68 L.9.c.a.b. and 1000 rds at aircraft. "D" Coy fired 10,000 rds on tracks F.29.c.20.60 Road L4.b., F.23.d 8.8 to F.2.a.c.15.90, F.23.d.5.0 to F.2.a.c 2 h. Casualties Nil.	
"	12		Activity normal. Visibility good. Aerial activity normal. "D" Coy fired 11000 rds in support of raid by 8th Queens Light Infantry(?)	

Army Form C. 2118.

WAR DIARY
or
INTELLIGENCE SUMMARY.
(Erase heading not required.)

Instructions regarding War Diaries and Intelligence Summaries are contained in F. S. Regs. Part II. and the Staff Manual respectively. Title pages will be prepared in manuscript.

Place	Date	Hour	Summary of Events and Information	Remarks and references to Appendices
BUCQUOY SECTOR			Reference map 1:20000 France sheet 57d N.E.	
	12		From 2.55 a.m. to 4 a.m.: Harassing fire was also carried out. "A" Coy fired 6500 rnds on Road L4 b 8, L4 c 80.20 to L9 b 06.90, L 8 a 2.6, L 9 a 5.3, and 210 rnds sniping. "D" Coy fired 15000 rnds on track F29 c 5.3 - F29 c 90.80, F29 d 55.35 to F29 a 92.92, F2Hc 13 to F2Hc 60.15, 290 rnds at aircraft and 60 rnds sniping. Casualties nil.	Ref. [illegible]
	13		Activity normal. A gas projector attack was successfully carried out on BUCQUOY sector (L9A) and our Machine Guns assisted "A" Company firing 1500 rnds on trench system on L9B, and "D" Coy fired 6000 rnds on trench system on L9A and L4B. Harassing fire was also carried out "A" Coy fired 5000 rnds on Road L4b, track L4c 80.85 to L9b 88.18 and Cross line L4c L9d, L8d L6, L9a 53 and 3d rnds sniping. "D" Coy fired 9000 rnds on track F2Hc 10.30 to F2Hc 60.15, area round L 5 b 18.92, track F29d 63.35 to F29d 92.82, and 250 rnds at aircraft. Visibility fair. Casualties nil.	Appendix I Report Ref. [illegible]
	14		Activity nothing on our side. Enemy quiet. Division on Right advanced their line owing to enemy's evacuation. Inflict hostile front and on our front. "A" Coy fired 5000 rnds on Road L9 b 66 to L9 a d 4b, Road L4c 65 to L4c 20.55, trench system L9A - L8a, and 150 rnds. at aircraft. "D" Coy fired 2500 rnds on Road F29b, F29a 5.10, light railway F29c 95 to F29d 3.5, and 600 rnds at aircraft. Visibility poor. Casualties nil.	Appendix II Report Ref. [illegible]
	15		Activity normal. At night "A" Coy were relieved by 101 Coy. who do so 0.4y. In conjunction with raid by 18th Bn. Northern Brigade "D" Coy fired 10000 rnds on track F29b C4 to F29a 3.3 and Road F8a 1.6 & F29a 9992. In conjunction with raid by Right battalion Worcester Brigade "D" Coy fired 8550 rnds on Road L4 b 92.45, track L4 b L9 31, and Trenches L10d. 250 rnds. were fired at aircraft. Visibility bad. Casualties nil.	Appendix III Report Ref. [illegible]
	16		Activity normal. Visibility good. "C" Coy fired 5000 rnds on L9 c 93, track L4 c 22 to L4 c 54, Road L4 c and trench at system to F 88. "D" Coy fired 9000 rnds on Road L4 b, track F29 c 26 to F29 c 10.25, F23a 80.10 Road and track system to F 88. F2Hc 20.10 and 100 rnds at aircraft. Aircraft activity normal. Casualties nil. to F2Hc 18.90, F23b 90.00 to F2Hc 20.10	Appendix IV Report Ref. [illegible]
	16		Activity normal. Visibility fair. "C" Coy fired 6000 rnds on L 4 b 9.5, L9 b 00.00 to L10 a 0.10, Road and tracks L 8 c d, D c b. "D" fired 6000 rnds on Trench F29d 53-36 - F29d 92.82, track function at L5 b 18.92, track F2Hc 10.30 to F2Hc 60.15, and 100 rnds on aircraft. Casualties nil.	Ref. [illegible]
	17			Ref. [illegible]

Army Form C. 2118.

WAR DIARY
or
INTELLIGENCE SUMMARY.
(Erase heading not required.)

Instructions regarding War Diaries and Intelligence Summaries are contained in F. S. Regs., Part II. and the Staff Manual respectively. Title pages will be prepared in manuscript.

Place	Date	Hour	Summary of Events and Information	Remarks and references to Appendices
Bucquoy Section				Reference Maps 1:20000 France Sheets 57D N.E. and 57C N.W.
	18		Activity normal. Visibility good. "C" Coy fired 6000 rds. on Road L14c4d, L10a45.55, L10c12.65. "D" Coy fired 6000 rds. on Lunch F29b30.50 & F29b yard, F30a95.65, track junction F29c90.50, and 250 rds. to M.G. emplacement. Casualties nil.	
	19		Enemy Quiet. Visibility fair. "D" Coy fired 12500 rds. on F29c95.53, tracks L14b90.25 to L5c30.40, F30a 95.65 and "C" Coy fired 8000 rds on L10a95.30, Road L14c4d, Area L10c. Enplacements dug and guns moved to new battery positions. Casualties nil.	
	20		Enemy Quiet entire day. At 4.55 a.m. our Inf. and Arms co-operated in attack by 31st Division on the high ground East of Bucquoy and ABLAINZEVILLE and ADINVAL 0.0.48. - Casualties - 1 O.R. wounded by shell fire.	
	21		Visibility not good. 31st Division gained objective and 63rd and 5th Divisions passed through. Tanks preceded Infantry. Afternoon Bn. moved - 63rd Division - A27A35, G3d3h, G9c.01, G3d.6.6. G6d20. 5th Division L9b50, G14c80, L24c9, L24c49, Visibility good after 9.30 a.m. Artillery very active on both sides. Enemy counter attacked unsuccessfully at 5 a.m. South of LOGEAST WOOD, ACHIET-LE-PETIT, IRLES - Casualties - 3 O.R. wounded by shell fire.	
	22		Companies remained in position during day. At night Division moved forward and relieved the 63rd Division. Infantry Bns. attached to Brigades as follows :- 13th (d) Bn. "D" Coy with 111th Inf. Bde. "B" Coy with 112th Inf. Bde. "A" Coy in Divisional Reserve. Casualties - 2 o.r. wounded.	
	23		37th Division attacked at 11 a.m. "D" Coy supported 111th Bde. in attack on ACHIET LE GRAND and BIHUCOURT, engaging enemy machine guns and following Infantry. Large numbers of enemy retiring in direction of SAPIGNIES - BIEFVILLERS - BEHAGNIES were engaged successfully. Enemy on SAPIGNIES - BIEFVILLERS road was also engaged. "B" Coy with 112th Bde. "C" Coy with 113th Bde. were...	

WAR DIARY or INTELLIGENCE SUMMARY.

Army Form C. 2118.

Place	Date	Hour	Summary of Events and Information	Remarks and references to Appendices
				Reference Maps 1:20000 France, Sheets 57/D N.E. and 57c N.W.
	23		Subject to 111th Bde. work orders to advance & infiltrate at places through if necessary. Casualties: 1 O.R. killed, 5 wounded. "B" Coy moved to LOGEAST WOOD Grid. 15.b.5.	
	24		13th Bty. Bde. now became forward Bde and took BIEFVILLERS. "C" Coy advanced and on reaching "A" Coy advanced, the remains of W.H. Infantry at BIEFVILLERS. 112th Bgde went into support and "B" Coy were concentrated in trench S.W. of BIHUCOURT. "A" Coy came forward and consolidated round ACHIET LEGRAND. Casualties – W.W. B.C.S. Johnson wounded, 1 O.R. killed, 13 wounded, and 1 missing.	
	25		At dawn the 63rd Bde. attacked the high ground traversed by the SAPIGNIES–BAPAUME Road. Was checked at C Coy advanced whose infantry about this portion catch up overland line. Platoon targets were suggest N.E. of FAVREUIL for several machines. The 111th Inf. Bde. attacked SAPIGNIES. "D" Coy co-operating. Bn. Cmdr. of "D" Coy went forward to ascertain he was given as it was noted that the 2nd Division had taken the village. At 6pm the 111 th Bde. attacked FAVREUIL. "D" Coy gave direct covering fire from ridge in front of ARRAS–BAPAUME Road. Good targets were obtained. "C" Coy also gave covering fire for this attack. Gestures will now available. "A" and "B" Coys remained in position. Casualties – 2/Lt Laurence killed, 2/Lt Pearse and 2/Lt Wilson Robert wounded, 2 o.r. killed, 11 wounded and 4 missing.	
	26		In the morning the 5th Bn. M.G.C. relieved this Battn. and Company proceeded to LOGEAST WOOD. L.6.a and C.whose dispositions are annotated. Casualties nil.	
	27/31		Battalion in billets in L.6.a and C. Training carried out. Advanced Bn. H.Q. with Divisions H.2. at Brickworks ACHIET LE GRAND. Casualties nil.	

Maj. Tuson Lt.Col.
Comdg. 3/1 Bn. I/16 H. Regt.

appendix 1

SECRET.   37th Battalion, Machine Gun Corps.   Copy No. 13.

Operation Order No. 45.

Ref. Map 57 B. N.E. 1/20,000.   2nd August 1918.

1. "D" Company, 37th Battalion, Machine Gun Corps will relieve "C" Company, in the Northern Brigade Group, on the night of the 5th/6th August.

2. Details of relief will be arranged between Company Commanders concerned.

3. On completion of the relief, O.C. "D" Company will take over the Command of the 20 guns of the Northern Brigade Group.

4. After relief, "C" Company will take over the present accommodation and duties of "D" Company.

5. Officers of "D" Company will reconnoitre the area beforehand, and one man per team of "D" Company will be attached to the corresponding teams of "C" Company for twenty four hours before relief.

6. All Maps, Defence Schemes, Trench Stores, Work proposed and in hand, and Gas clothing, will be carefully handed over and copies of receipts sent to this office within 24 hours of relief.

7. Completion of relief will be wired to this office by code word "SPIRIT".

8. Acknowledge. (M.G.Units only)

Issued at 6 pm

R H Peacock
Captain,
Adjutant, 37th Battn. Machine Gun Corps.

Copies to:-
1. 37th Division. "G".
2. 63rd Infantry Brigade.
3. 111th   "   "
4. 112th   "   "
5. 2nd Battalion. M.G.C.
6. 37th Div. Sig. Co. R.E.
7. "A" Company.
8. "B" Company.
9. "C"   "
10. "D"   "
11. Signal Officer.
12. Quartermaster.
13/14. War Diary.
15. File.

Appendix 2

SECRET.   **37th BATTALION. MACHINE GUN CORPS.**   Copy No. 11.

Operation Order No.46.

11th August 1918.

Ref.Map 57.D. N.E. 1/20,000.

1. A projector attack will be carried out on the enemy trench system S.E. of BUCQUOY on 12th August or on the first morning after that on which weather conditions are favourable.

2. Projectors have been installed at F.27.c.30.15.

3. The following targets have been selected:-
    L.3.b.15.50.
    L.3.b.35.75.
    L.3.b.62.88.
    L.3.b.90.93.

4. The following code words will be in use :-
    CABBAGE.   "Weather conditions are unfavourable and discharge is postponed 24 hours."

    POTATO.   "Weather conditions are favourable and preliminary arrangements for discharge will be made."

    KIDNEY.   "Weather conditions remain favourable and discharge will take place."

    ROSES.   "Projectors have been successfully discharged."

5. O.C. "O" Special Coy. R.E. will finally decide whether weather conditions are favourable or not and he will send Code messages direct to :-
    Right Brigade Headquarters.
    Left Brigade Headquarters.
    Left Battn. Right Brigade.

6. Artillery and Machine Guns will co-operate.

7. Machine Guns will co-operate as follows:-
   Right Group. 4 guns.
   Zero plus 20 - zero plus 40.   Bursts of fire 75 rnds. per minute on Targets as given in para.3 and trench system in L.3.b.

   Left Group. 4 guns.
   Zero plus 20 - zero plus 40.   Trench systems in L.10.a. & L.4.c. Bursts of fire of 75 rnds. per min.

8. Watches will be synchronised at 112th Infantry Brigade Headquarters at 10.0 p.m. on 11th August.

9. Zero hour will be 6.0 a.m. on 12th August.

10. No reference to this operation will be made over the telephone.

        Issued at 9.0 a.m.

                                R.Peacock
                                                Captain,
                        Adjutant, 37th Battn. Machine Gun Corps.

COPIES TO:-

   No.1. 37th Division "G".   No.7. "C" Company.
      2. 63rd Infantry Brigade.   8. Signalling Officer.
      3. 112th Infantry Brigade.   9/10. File.
      4. "A" Company.   11/12. War Diary.
      5. "B"   "

Appendix VIII

SECRET.   37th Battalion. Machine Gun Corps.   Copy No. 11

Operation Order No. 47.

Ref.Map. 57.B. N.E. 1/20,000.   14th August 1918.
         57.C. N.W.   do.

1. Prisoners captured today state that the enemy has withdrawn to his main line of resistance on the general line L.8.d.0.0. - L.4.central - F.28.c.8.5.

2. In the event of an enemy withdrawal patrols supported by other troops are to be pushed forward,
   (a) to maintain touch with the enemy.
   (b) to make good any ground valuable to us.

3. Forward movement will be by bounds with the general object of establishing a line of observation on the following approximate line:
   First Line. (RED) L.9.central - L.4.central - F.28.a.2.0. - F.29.c.6.0. - F.29.b.4.6.
   Second Line. (BROWN) L.10.d.5.6. - L.11.a.4.4. - L.5.b.5.0. - F.30.a.0.0. - F.24.a.5.0. - F.24.a.3.5.
   Third Line. (BLUE) L.12.c.2.6. - L.6.c.7.4. - F.30.c.7.0. - A.25.a.0.6. - A.19.b.8.2.

4. (a) Machine Gun Group Commanders will keep closely in touch with the Brigades to which they are attached.
   (b) In the event of the BLUE line being attained the present line of observation will become the main line of resistance.
   (c) Any guns that have to be moved forward will be moved from guns at present in and behind the PURPLE System and if necessary from the FONQUEVILLERS GROUP. The new and old positions of any guns moved will be notified to H.Q. immediately.
   (d) "C" Company will be under one hour's notice to move.
   (e) Communication will be from front to rear.

Issued at 11.0 p.m.

                                         R.H.Hedcock   Captain,
                              Adjutant, 37th Batta. Machine Gun Corps.

Copies to :-

   1. 37th Division. "G".   7. "B" Company.
   2. 62rd Inf. Bde.   8. Signal Officer.
   3. 112th " "   9/10. File.
   4. "A" Company.   11/12. War Diary.
   5. "B"   "
   6. "C"   "

SECRET.   37th BATTALION, MACHINE GUN CORPS. Copy No. 13.

Appendix IV

Operation Order No. 47.

11th August 1918.

Ref.Map. 57 D. N.E. 1/20,000.

1. "C" Company, 37th Battalion, Machine Gun Corps, will relieve "A" Company in the Southern Brigade Group on the Night of 15th/16th August.

2. Details of relief will be arranged between the Company Commanders concerned.

3. On completion of relief, O.C. "C" Company will take over the Command of the 20 guns of the Southern Brigade Group.

4. After relief, "A" Company will take over the present accommodation and duties of "C" Company.

5. Officers of "C" Company will reconnoitre the area beforehand and one man per team of "C" Company will be attached to corresponding teams of "A" Company for twentyfour hours before relief.

6. All maps, Defence Schemes, Trench Stores, Work proposed and in hand, and Gas Clothing, will be carefully handed over, and receipts sent to this office within 24 hours of relief.

7. Completion of relief will be wired to this office by use of the Code word "RECEIVED".

8. Acknowledge. (M.G.Units only).

Issued at 6.0 p.m.

T. Thomson
Captain,
Adjutant, 37th Battn. Machine Gun Corps.

Copies to :-

1. 37th Division "G".
2. 63rd Inf. Bde.
3. 111th " "
4. 112th " "
5. N.Z. Bn. M.G.C.
6. 37th Div.Sig.Co. R.E.
7. "A" Company.
8. "B" Company.
9. "C" "
10. "D" "
11. Signal Officer.
12. Q.M.
13/14. War Diary.
15. File.

SECRET.

M.G. 249.

AMENDMENT TO 37th BATTN. M.G. CORPS
Operation Order No. 47.

Cancel sub.para.(b) of para.4 and substitute :-

When a line of observation is established on the BLUE Line, the line of resistance would then probably be a series of strong points to be constructed on the reverse slope of the crest immediately West of the RED Line.

R. Richards
Captain,
Adjutant, 37th Battn. Machine Gun Corps.

15th August 1918.

Issued to all recipients of above order dated 14th August 1918.

Appendix V

SECRET.　　　　　37th BATTALION. MACHINE GUN CORPS.　　　Copy No. 12

Operation Order No. 48.

Ref. Maps 57D N.E.) 1/20,000.　　　　　　　　19th August 1918.
　　　　　　57C N.W.)

1.　　The Division is to capture and consolidate in depth the high ground East of BUCQUOY and ABLAINZEVILLE at an early date.

2.　　The N.Z. Division are to co-operate on the right by securing the general line L.14.central - L.9.central.
　　The 2nd Division are attacking on the left with the object of establishing a line of observation on the general line F.24.a.0.5. - A.8.a.0.0. - A.3.a.0.0.

3.　　The attack will be carried out by the 63rd Infantry Brigade on the right and the 111th Infantry Brigade on the left.
　　The 112th Infantry Brigade less two Battalions will be in Divisional Reserve.

4.　　The objective will be the enemy main line of resistance L.9.central - L.4.b.4.2. - F.29.a.2.0. - F.29.a.9.5. - F.29.b.5.5. thence F.24.c.0.0. - F.24.a.5.5.
　　Patrols will be pushed forward to the general line L.9.d.1.6. - L.10.a.4.6. - L.4.b.9.3. - F.29.c.0.0. - F.29.b.0.0. - F.29.b.7.0. - F.24.c.3.0. - A.19.b.9.4.

5.　　The attack will be made under a creeping barrage of Field and Heavy Artillery and under a Machine Gun Barrage.
　　Tanks will co-operate.

6.　　Machine Guns will co-operate as follows :-
(a) Right Group. (Commander - Maj.F.J.Beechman) 5 Batteries of present Right Brigade Group and one battery of FONQUEVILLERS Group attached, will place a standing frontal barrage as follows:-
"A" Battery.　　L.10.d.6.4. - L.10.d.95.95.
"B"　"　　　　L.10.d.95.95. - L.11.a.20.48.
"C"　"　　　　L.11.a.20.48. - L.5.c.40.10.
"D"　"　　　　L.5.c.40.10. - L.5.c.50.60.
"E"　"　　　　L.5.c.70.55. - L.5.a.95.06.
"F"　"　　　　L.5.a.95.06. - L.5.b.16.66.
　　Group Hd.Qrs. at Right Inf. Bde. Hd.Qrs.
　　All batteries 4 guns each.

(b) Left Group. (Commander - Maj.V.A.Tylor) - 5 Batteries of present Left Brigade Group and one battery of FONQUEVILLERS Group attached, will place a standing frontal barrage as follows:-
"G" Battery.　　L.5.b.50.66. - F.29.d.56.22.
"H"　"　　　　F.29.d.80.10. - F.29.d.80.65.
"I"　"　　　　F.30.c.00.10. - F.30.c.00.60.
"J"　"　　　　F.30.c.00.72. - F.30.c.70.70.
"K"　"　　　　F.30.c.82.57. - F.30.a.85.12.
"L"　"　　　　A.25.a.11.10. - A.25.a.25.60.
　　Group Hd.Qrs. at Left Inf. Bde. Hd.Qrs.
　　All batteries 4 guns each.

(c) Forward Group (Commander - Capt.S.W.Chater, M.C.) will work in two sub.-groups - one with Right Brigade and the other with Left Brigade.
　　Left Sub.-Group will assemble in ABLAIN trench (F.28.b.) and ROCKET Trench (F.22.b.)
　　Right Sub.-Group will assemble in Western outskirts of BUCQUOY.
　　Sub.-Groups will move forward with Infantry until clear of enemy barrage and will then wait until Infantry have attained their objectives when they will move forward to approximate positions as shown on attached trace.

A11

-2-

All guns to be sited to fire direct.
Main tasks have already been allotted to the guns.
Group Hd.Qrs. will be near Right Inf. Bde. Hd.Qrs. with an Officer near Left Inf. Bde. Hd.Qrs.

(d) N.Z.Battery (KIWI) of 8 guns will assist as follows :-
Zero to Zero plus 10 minutes on trench L.9.b.10.68. to L.9.b.70.95.
At Zero plus 10 minutes will search the double line of trenches from L.9.b.55.85. to L.9.b.70.95. lifting 100 yards every 4 minutes until fire rests on the open from Communication trench L.10.a.80.00 to L.10.a.90.10. to the Communication trench L.10.d.72.78. to L.10.d.80.90.
Rate of fire. Zero to Zero plus 10 mins.   100 rds. per min.
Zero Plus 10 mins. to Zero plus 60. 50 rds. per min.

(e) Times and rates of fire for Right and Left Groups :-
Zero to Zero plus 10 mins.   100 rds. per min.
Zero plus 10 mins. to Zero plus 60 mins.   50 "   "   "
Zero plus 80 "   " Zero plus 84 "   100 "   "   "
Zero plus 84 "   " Zero plus 92 "   50 "   "   "

(f) S.O.S.
Batteries of Right and Left Groups with the exception of "P" Battery will take the standing barrage as given in (a) and (b) as their S.O.S. Lines.
"P" Battery will take L.11.a.50.75. to L.5.c.75.10. as its S.O.S. Line.
Rate of fire for S.O.S. will be 200 rounds per minute for 2 minutes then 50 rounds per minute until "all quiet."

(g) Attached trace shows :-
    (a) Barrage and S.O.S. Lines.
    (b) Approximate final positions of forward guns.

7.   Zero date and hour will be notified later.

8.   Instructions regarding communications, synchronisation, reports, supplies, etc. will be issued later.

9.   Acknowledge
                Issued at 11.30 p.m.

                                        Captain,
                        Adjutant, 37th Battn. Machine Gun Corps.

Distribution :-
    1. 37th Division. "Q".   7. "C" Company.
    2. 63rd Inf. Bde.   8. "D" Company.
    3. 111th Inf. Bde.   9. N.Z. M.G. Battalion.
    4. 112th Inf. Bde.   10. 37th D.A.
    5. "A" Company.   11. Signalling Officer.
    6. "B" Company.   12/13. War Diary.
                14. File.

SECRET.   M.G.253.

INSTRUCTIONS NOS. 1 and 2.

(Supplementary to 37th Bn.M.G.C. Order No.48.)

1. **Communications.**

   Direct telephone lines are laid and will be maintained from each Battery to its Group Hd.Qrs. and thence back to Division etc. by Brigade Lines.
   Location of Batteries :-
   Left Group.   "G" Battery.   F.27.a.5.1.81.
                  "H"   "   F.21.d.8.6.
                  "I" & "J" Batteries.   F.23.a.7.0.
                  "K" & "L"   "   F.23.a.0.3.
   Right Group.   "A" "B" & "C" Batteries.   L.2.d.
                  "D" "E" & "F"   "   F.27.a.

   Machine Gun Battalion Advanced Report Centre will be established at present Left Bdn. H.Q. - LA BRAYELLE FARM E.23.d.8.5.60.
   The Signalling Officer and 3 O.R. with cycles will constitute personnel there.

   Communications between forward guns and Sub.-Group H.Q. will be by runner until situation permits of wires being laid.

2. **Miscellaneous.**

   (a) Harassing Fire.
   Normal harassing fire will be carried out on Y/Z night especially between Zero minus 1 hour and Zero, so as to cover the forward movement of Tanks.
   (b) Other Troops.
   5th and 63rd Divisions will commence passing through our forward line (BLUE dotted line) at Zero plus 90.
   (c) Synchronisation.
   Code word "RIGHT" will be wired to Groups.
   On receipt of this wire Group Commanders will send an Officer to Brigade Hd.Qrs. to ascertain arrangements for synchronisation.
   (d) Tracing "D" is issued to Groups herewith. Tracing "D" shows enemy dispositions and direction of possible counter-attacks.
   (e) Troops will not show themselves during the day of 20th August.
   (f) White Very Lights will be fired by leading troops of 63rd and 111th Infantry Brigades on reaching the enemy main line of resistance i.e. BLUE Line.

                                                  Captain,
                              Adjutant, 37th Battn. Machine Gun Corps.
20th August 1918.

              Issued to all recipients of 37th Bn.M.G.C. Operation
              Order No.48 d/19/8/18.

Appendix VI

SECRET.

37th Division. "G".	63rd Inf. Bde.	M.G. 257.
"A" Company.	111th " "	
"B" "	112th " "	
"C" "	O.C. Signals.	
"D" "		

1. The Division is moving up tonight 22/23, and taking up a battle formation on the line at present held by 63rd Division.

2. Machine Gun Companies will co-operate with Infantry Brigades as follows :-
   "C" Company with 63rd Inf. Bde.
   "D" "   "   111th "   "
   "B" "   "   112th "   "
Companies will move under orders to be issued by Brigades and subsequent co-operation to be arranged between Company Commanders and Brigades.

3. "A" Company will be in Divisional Reserve and will remain in positions of assembly in vicinity of TOP Trench. Further orders will be issued to "A" Company.

4. Role of Machine Guns.
   (a) To help Infantry forward at all stages of the advance by bringing fire to bear on any enemy holding them up.
   (b) After the advance consolidation in depth of ground gained.
   (c) Some guns to be pushed forward under a covering party to bring direct fire to bear on enemy until Infantry pass through them.
   (d) Direct overhead fire to be employed if possible.

5. Advanced Battalion Hd.Qrs. will be with Advanced Division. Location notified later.

22nd August 1918.

R. Peacock. Captain,
Adjutant, 37th Battn. Machine Gun Corps.

37th Bn Machine Gun Corps.

War Diary
for the
month of September 1916.

WAR DIARY
or
INTELLIGENCE SUMMARY.

(Erase heading not required.)

Army Form C. 2118.

Lieut-Col
Commanding 37th Bn. Machine Gun. Corps

SEPTEMBER 1918.

Place	Date	Hour	Summary of Events and Information	Remarks and references to Appendices
			Reference map 1:20000 France Sheet and 1:40000 sheet 57C	
	1		Battalion in tents and shelters in L 6 A and C. Training carried out. Rear Battalion H.2. at 5.16.2.4. Advanced Battalion H.2. with Division at old Brickworks, ACHIET LE GRAND. Casualties nil.	Ref I
	2		Battalion in tents and shelters at LOGEAST WOOD (L 6 a and c) - Training carried out. Battalion H.2 at Brickworks ACHIET LE GRAND. Casualties nil.	Ref I
	3		Division moved forward to relieve 5th Division. Companies were attached to Brigades as follows:- "A" Company with 111th Bde.; "B" Coy with 112th Bde.; "C" Coy with 63rd Bde.; and "D" Coy in Divisional Reserve. 112th Bde. went into front line. 63rd Bde. were in support and "C" Coy went into bivouacs S.W. of LEBUCQUIERE. 111th Bde. was in reserve and area in FAVREUIL area. "D" Coy moved to FAVREUIL. Advanced Battalion moved and Advanced H.Q. to FAVREUIL, and Rear Bn. H.Q. with Rear Echelons moved to BIHUCOURT. Casualties - 1 O.R. wounded.	Ref 8
	4		111th Bde. got into touch with the enemy and the sections of "B" Coy. were pushed forward and attached to Infantry Battalions. 63rd Bde. moved up in support. Sections of "C" Coy. being attached to coast infantry. "A" Coy with 111th Bde. in FAVREUIL area. "D" Coy in FAVREUIL. Rear Bn. H.Q. moved to FAVREUIL. "C" Coy hat echelon moved to BEUGNY and "B" Coy rear echelon to LEBUCQUIERE. Casualties - 1 O.R. killed, 2 O.R. wounded. 4 mules wounded. 2 of which were destroyed.	Ref 8
	5		The Hun became more stable, guns of "B" Coy were moved further forward and line of defence taken up along sunken road in J 29 c and J 35 a. At night the enemy attempted to hand out	Ref 8

Army Form C. 2118.

WAR DIARY
or
INTELLIGENCE SUMMARY.
(Erase heading not required.)

Lieut.-Col. Commanding 37th Bn. Machine Gun Corps.

SEPTEMBER 1918

Place	Date	Hour	Summary of Events and Information	Remarks and references to Appendices
	5		"B" Coy. brought guns into action at seen off. The 63rd Bde. were ordered to take over the line of the Battalion front on the right. "A" Coy in FAVREUIL area. "D" Coy in FAVREUIL. Battalion H.Q. in FAVREUIL. Casualties: 1 O.R. killed, 9 O.R. wounded.	CRBW
	6		The machine section of "C" Coy. was moved up in support of the 8th Somerset Light Infantry which continued to move forward through HAVRINCOURT WOOD. Coy. O.C. and O.2.a. 2 guns of "B" Coy. were moved to SQUARE CB56 in K25d and 2 guns into the Sunken Lane in YORKSHIRE BANK in K32.a.: "A" Coy with 111th Bde. in FAVREUIL area. "D" Coy in FAVREUIL. Battalion H.Q. in FAVREUIL: Casualties: 1 O.R. wounded.	CRBW
	7		"C" Coy joined in advance through HAVRINCOURT WOOD. Front quieter. Guns of "C" Coy were placed to cover BANBURY HILL, HAVRINCOURT, and waters cuts from the wood. "A" Coy with 111th Bde. in FAVREUIL area. "D" Coy in FAVREUIL. Battalion H.Q. in FAVREUIL. Casualties - NIL.	CRBW
	8		Situation unchanged. Casualties - NIL.	
	9		At night the 63rd Brigade took over the Divisional front. Two sections of "B" Coy were retained on the line, and along with "C" Coy were attached to the 63rd Brigade. The remainder of "B" Coy withdrew with the 112th Bde. to the LEBUCQUIERE area. "A" Coy with the 111th Brigade moved to the area about BERTINCOURT and took over defence of the main line of resistance. P.2.d. - J.33 central. - J.24 central. "D" Coy in FAVREUIL: Battalion H.Q. in FAVREUIL.	CRBW
FAVREUIL	10		2 guns of "C" Coy moved to Q.36.B.82 where they commanded TRESCAULT VALLEY and the high ground in Q.S. including BILHEM FM. Casualties:- 1 O.R. wounded	CRBW

WAR DIARY
or
INTELLIGENCE SUMMARY.

Army Form C. 2118.

Lieut-Col. Commanding 37th Bn. Machine Gun. Corps.

SEPTEMBER 1918

Place	Date	Hour	Summary of Events and Information	Remarks and references to Appendices
VELU WOOD	SEPT. 11 & 12		Bn. H.Qrs. moved to VELU WOOD in the afternoon. The two sections of 'B' Coy. in the line were withdrawn to LEBUCQUIERE area & Rationed (12 guns) of 'C' Coy. were withdrawn from the line between 1 am. & 4 am to LEBUCQUIERE area. Remaining section of 'C' Coy. remained in position in front of TUNNEL AVENUE. These guns moved to advance of the 111th Inf. Bde. at dawn on the morning of the 12th. This section of 'C' Coy. H.Qrs. moved back to LEBUCQUIERE area later on in the morning. 'A' Coy. was att. to 111th Inf. Bde. for the attack on the morning 12th inst. The 16 guns of 'A' Coy. were disposed as follows:- 2 guns att. 13th K.R.R.C. 4 guns att. 13th R.B. 8 guns barrage. Remaining 4 guns in reserve at western edge of HAVRINCOURT WOOD P.12.c.80.66. During the above operations 'D' Coy. was att. to 112th Bde (in support) in Railway Junction near BERTIN COURT. Casualties :- 2 O.R. killed; 10 Officers, 15 O.R. wounded.	CRBW
"	13		Disposition Bn. H.Qrs. and Coys. same as 12th inst. 2 guns of 'A' Coy. fired a portion of enemy during counter attack. Casualties:- 1 O.R. killed 6 OR. wounded.	CRBW
"	14		Disposition as on 13th inst. Casualties :- nil.	CRBW
"	15		'A' Coy. relieved by 'D' Coy. in the line. 'A' Coy. moved back in support in BERTIN COURT area. Casualties :- nil	Appendices I CRBW
"	16		'C' Coy. moved up to BERTINCOURT (support) area with 63rd Inf. Bde and relieved 'A' Coy. which moved back to LEBUCQUIERE (reserve) area with 111th Bde. No other change in disposition. Casualties:- nil	CRBW
"	17		1 Section of 'B' Coy. moved up to the line from LEBUCQUIERE area and was att. to 'D' Coy. Casualties :- 1 O.R. wounded.	CRBW
"	18		'D' Coy. assisted in the repulse of a strong enemy attack in the afternoon. 'C' Coy. was moved up with 63rd Bde. returning at about 9 p.m. on the 19th inst. G.O.C. congratulated 'D' Coy. for the part they had taken in the repulse of the enemy attack.	CRBW

WAR DIARY
or
INTELLIGENCE SUMMARY.

(Erase heading not required.) SEPTEMBER 1918

Army Form C. 2118.

Lieut-Col.
Commanding 37th Bn. Machine Gun. Corps.

Place	Date	Hour	Summary of Events and Information	Remarks and references to Appendices
VEL U WOOD	19		No change in dispositions. Casualties 5 O.R. wounded.	CRBW.
"	20		On the night of the 20th D.Coy & 1 section of "B"Coy in the line were relieved by "D" Coy. 42nd Bn. M.G.C. "D" Coy. 37th Bn. M.G.C. after relief went back by lorry to LE BARQUE area. Casualties: nil.	CRBW
LE BARQUE	21.		Bn. H.Qrs "B" & "C" Coys. relieved by 42nd Bn. M.G.C. moved back to rest area. Bn. H.Q. & "B" Coy. to LE BARQUE area. "C" Coy. to PYS area. Casualties: nil.	CRBW
"	22		"A" Coy moved back in the morning to PYS area. Casualties - nil.	CRBW.
"	23 & 24		These days were spent in training, cleaning up etc.	CRBW.
"	25.		A, C & D Coys. carried on with training programme. "B" Coy was att. to 5th R.M.G. and moved up to ROYAULCOURT.	CRBW.
"	26		A, C & D Coys. carried on with training. On the night of / the 26/27 B"Coy prepared battery position in front of HAVRINCOURT WOOD. Casualties nil. 11,700 rounds were fired.	CRBW
"	27		"B" Coy covered the advance of the 5th Div from 7:52 a.m. - 11:20 a.m. B"Coy remained in S.O.S. line for the rest of the day. Casualties: 9 O.R. wounded. A, C & D Coys. carried on with training programme.	CRBW
"	28		The enemy were driven back in the morning and B Coy moved back to ROYAULCOURT. A, C & D Coy training Casualties: nil.	CRBW
"	29.		A, C, & D. H.Q. Coys. Church parade. Rd.inspections etc. B" Coy. moved back to LE BARQUE area. Casualties: nil. In the afternoon which A Coy. which was att. to 111th Bgde. moved forward to VILLERS au - FLOS.	CRBW.

Army Form C. 2118.

WAR DIARY
or
INTELLIGENCE SUMMARY.

Commanding 37th Bn. Machine Gun Corps.

(Erase heading not required.) SEPTEMBER 1918

Place	Date	Hour	Summary of Events and Information	Remarks and references to Appendices
LE BARQUE	29 (continued)		"C" Coy, which was att. to 112th Inf. Bde. moved forward to BEUGNY area.	CRB 34
BERTINCOURT	30		Bn. H.Q. "B" & "D" Coys. moved forward to BERTINCOURT area. "A" Coy, which was still att. to 111 Bde. moved forward to East of GOUZEAUCOURT to relieve the forward brigade of the 5th Division. "C" Coy. remained att. to 112th Bde. which moved forward to relieve the support brigade of the 5th Division in the GOUZEAUCOURT WOOD area. Casualties: nil.	Appendices II CRBW

Referenced by
L. F. J. Coy
Aug 30

SECRET.

37th Battalion, Machine Gun Corps.

Operation Order No.49.

13th Sept.1918.

1. "D" Company, 37th Battn.Machine Gun Corps will relieve "A" Company 37th Battn.Machine Gun Corps on the night of the 14th/15th Sept.1918.

2. O.C. "D" Company will proceed to "A" Company Hd.Qrs. (P.11.b.10.25.) on the morning of the 14th inst. and arrange details of relief with O.C. "A" Company.

3. On relief "A" Company will withdraw to positions at present occupied by "D" Company.

4. Relief complete will be reported to this office.

Lieut.-Colonel,
Commanding 37th Battn.Machine Gun Corps.

Copies to :-
1. 37th Division "G".
2. 63rd Inf. Bde.
3. 111th Inf. Bde.
4. "A" Coy. Advd.
5. "A" Coy. Rear.
6. "D" Coy. Advd.
7. "D" Coy. Rear.
8. Quartermaster.
9/10. War Diary.
11. File.

appendix II

SECRET.   Copy No. 9

37TH BATTALION, MACHINE GUN CORPS.
ORDER NO. 22.

Ref. Map 57 C. 1/40,000.   30th Sept. 1918.

1.   "B" Company, "D" Company and Bn. Hd. Qrs. will move forward tomorrow 1st October.
   (a) "B" Company will move off at 10.45 a.m. and will take over the accommodation of the corresponding M.G. Company of the 5th Bn. M.G.C. in area Q.13.d. and Q.14.c.
   (b) "D" Company will move off at 10.50 a.m. and will take over accommodation from corresponding M.G.Company of 5th Bn. M.G.C. at Q.20.d.25.25.
   (c) Bn. Hd. Qrs. will move off at 11.00 a.m. and will take over accommodation of Rear Bn. Hd. Qrs. of 5th Bn. M.G.C. at NEUVILLE-BOURJONVAL.

2.   Bn. Hd. Qrs. and Companies will send forward an Officer early tomorrow morning to take over accommodation.

3.   Advanced Bn. Hd. Qrs. will be at Q.20.d.2.4.

4.   Completion of move will be notified to Advanced Bn. Hd. Qrs.

   Issued at 8.0 p.m.

                                           R. Peacock Captain,
                                    Adjt. 37th Battn. Machine Gun Corps.

Distribution :-
   1. "A" Company.   6. Medical Officer.
   2. "B" Company.   7. Signalling Officer.
   3. "C" Company.   8. File.
   4. "D" Company.   9/10. War Diary.
   5. Quartermaster.

Vol 8

87th Bn Machine Gun Corps.

War Diary

for the month of October 1918

WAR DIARY or INTELLIGENCE SUMMARY.

Army Form C. 2118.

OCTOBER, 1918.

Reference Maps France, Sheets 57c S.E. & 57b S.W.
1:20000

Date	Hour	Summary of Events and Information	Remarks
1		The enemy had taken up defensive positions along the line of the ESCAUT CANAL and fresh was established there with him. The Guns of "A" Company (working in conjunction with the 111th Brigade) were disposed along the line of the VILLERS (GUISLAIN) – BONAVIS – CAMBRAI road between GOUZEAUCOURT and BONAVIS and were later brought up to the Western banks of the Canal. "C" Company (in conjunction with the 112th Brigade) was in close support in FIFTEEN RAVINE, north of GOUZEAUCOURT. "B" and "D" Companies were in reserve between HAVRINCOURT WOOD and (GOUZEAUCOURT RESERVE). "A" Company under orders of 63rd Brigade and "D" Company in Divisional Reserve. Advanced M.G. Battalion H.2. was established with H.2. 111th Brigade S.W. of LANECQUERIE. Casualties nil.	
2		Companies located as on 1st. Casualties 1 ot wounded.	
3		Guns of "A" Company moved to positions in LATEAU TRENCH, PELICAN AVENUE, and QUARRY POST. and fired on enemy approaches, suspected posts etc. Casualties – 3 o.t. wounded.	
4		At night the enemy retired to the MASNIERES – BEAUREVOIR line. Casualties nil.	
5		"D" Company went out through "A" Company and took up positions on the Eastern side of CHENEAUX WOOD and around CHENEAUX COPSE, VAUCELLES COPSE, and FOX FARM. – "A" Company then became Company in close support with 111th Brigade. – "C" Company moved up to the area around BLEAK HOUSE with 112th Brigade and "B" Company moved up to FIFTEEN AVENUE and remained in reserve with 63rd Brigade. Casualties nil.	

Army Form C. 2118.

WAR DIARY
or
INTELLIGENCE SUMMARY.
(Erase heading not required.) OCTOBER, 1918.

Place	Date	Hour	Summary of Events and Information	Remarks and references to Appendices
			References maps - France, Sheets 57c S.E. & 57b S.W. 1:20000	
	6		Advanced Battalion H.Q. moved forward with the 111th Brigade to the ravine west of VAUCELLES COPSE. Companies located as on 5th. Casualties - nil.	
	7		At night "A" Company moved up to positions of assembly in VAUCELLES COPSE, "C" Company moved up to positions of assembly in CHENEAUX WOOD, while "B" Company remaining in reserve, moved up to VAUCELLES and later to VAUCELLES WOOD. "D" Company remained in positions as on 5th. Casualties - 1 O.R. wounded.	
	8		At 05.10 hours the attack on the MASNIERES - BEAUREVOIR line was launched by the 112th Brigade, with 111th Brigade in Support, and 63rd Brigade in Reserve, and was completely successful. BEL AISE, BOIS PELU, LA PETITE MAISON, HURTEBISE FARM and the whole of BRISEUX WOOD except the South East corner being captured. "D" Company guns fired a creeping barrage to assist the advancing infantry, and were then collected and prepared to advance in neighbourhood of FOX FARM. "C" Company's guns accompanied the infantry and assisted in gaining fire superiority. Motor transport was engaged by direct fire on the road north of ESNES and put to flight and a hostile battery north east of BRISEAUX WOOD was forced to gallop back without coming into action. Numerous small parties of enemy were also successfully dealt with. "A" and "C" Companies supported an attack by the 63rd Brigade at 18.00 hours on the South Eastern corner of BRISEAUX WOOD where the enemy were making a stiff resistance. Casualties. 5 O.R. wounded.	

Army Form C. 2118.

WAR DIARY
or
INTELLIGENCE SUMMARY.
(Erase heading not required.)

OCTOBER, 1918.

Place	Date	Hour	Summary of Events and Information	Remarks and references to Appendices
			Reference maps 1:40000 France Sheet 57B. maps 1:20000 France Sheets 57B S.W., N.W., N.E.	
	9		The advance was resumed at 05.00 hours by the 63rd Brigade and continued by the 112th Brigade with the 111th Brigade in reserve. HAVRINCOURT and LIGNY were captured. Enemy held railway south and south-west of CAUDRY, and by the evening our line was approximately 700 yards south of and parallel to the railway. "A" Company covered the advance by indirect overhead fire until the safety limit was reached and they afterwards took up positions about HAVRINCOURT. Two sections of "C" Company went forward with the 63rd Brigade and came into positions in the sheet about 1000 yards due south of HAVRINCOURT CEMETERY. Two guns were moved forward to the outskirts of LIGNY where successful fire was brought to bear upon enemy troops retreating along the CAUDRY - MONTIGNY road, numerous casualties being inflicted. The 112th Brigade having now advanced through the 63rd Brigade, these two sections advanced first to the N.W. outskirts of CAUDRY. One section advanced with 1st Essex Regiment and successfully engaged a hostile machine gun seen firing from a house in the South Western outskirts of CAUDRY. The remaining section advanced with the 11/2nd Herts Regiment and getting into positions in the sunken road from LIGNY to FONTAINE, successfully engaged direct targets of enemy infantry along the railway between the LIGNY - CAUDRY road and the MONTIGNY - CAUDRY road. Retreating fire was maintained along the railway and southern outskirts of CAUDRY and enemy fire kept down. This Company's guns consolidated in depth the ground captured. "A", "B" and "D" Coys were moved up into HAVRINCOURT and the area immediately South thereof, and remained in Divisional Reserve. Casualties - Lt. J. Walker wounded, 3 o.r. wounded.	Photo [?]
	10		The advance was resumed at 05.00 hours by the 112th Brigade, the 63rd Brigade going through them later in the day, while the 111th Brigade remained in reserve. CAUDRY was found to have been evacuated and AUDENCOURT, BÉTHENCOURT and VIESLY were cleared of the enemy. Our line was	

WAR DIARY or INTELLIGENCE SUMMARY.

Army Form C. 2118.

OCTOBER, 1918.

Reference Map 1:40000 France - Sheet 57 b.
Map 1:20000 France - Sheet 57 b N.E.

Place	Date	Hour	Summary of Events and Information	Remarks and references to Appendices
	10		established along the Western bank of the river SELLE between BRIASTRE and NEUVILLY, but several posts of Germans remained in each village. Platoons of "C" Company swept the Southern and North Western outskirts of CAUDRY while the Infantry advanced by the South Eastern end of the town. Later they were collected and moved forward to consolidate the line BETHENCOURT - BEAUMONT - INCHY. "B" Coy working in conjunction with the 63rd Brigade advanced through the grounds of CLERMOYNT CHATEAU, knocking out three enemy machine guns in an apathy about 1600 yards N.W. of the CHATEAU and dispersing a considerable body of enemy Infantry on the crest of the ridge West of the River SELLE took up platoons of consolidation along the sunken roads on the top of the ridge. From here direct targets across the river were successfully engaged till dark. "A" Company moved forward into posts in BETHENCOURT, "D" Company moved into posts at AVDENCOURT and "C" Company remained in positions of consolidation as above. Casualties - Lieut. Forsyth and 2 o.r. killed.	
	11		During the morning the whole of the Western bank of the river was cleared of the enemy by the 63rd Brigade, and later in the day infantry patrols were pushed across the stream and the process of bridging was commenced. Our Section of "B" Coy on the forward slope West of the river fired during the day at several targets which appeared on the rising ground East of the Railway as opportunity arose and several casualties were seen to be inflicted. Two sections of Middlesex moved into positions of assembly on the Eastern bank of the river together with one Section of "D" Company in the night and one Section of "A" Company on the left. The remainder of "A" and "D" Coys remained as on 10th while "C" Coy was withdrawn into billets in CAUDRY and remained in Divisional Reserve. Casualties - Lt. Bowman and 8 o.r. wounded.	
	12		The attack was resumed at 05.10 hours by the 4th Middlesex together with one Section of "A" Company and one Section of "D" Company. The Railway was crossed and the Infantry gained the crest of the ridge,	

Army Form C. 2118.

WAR DIARY
or
INTELLIGENCE SUMMARY.
(Erase heading not required.) OCTOBER, 1918.

Place	Date	Hour	Summary of Events and Information	Remarks and references to Appendices
	12		Reference - Map - France, Sheet 57 B N.E. 1:20000. East of the river. From the forward slope of the ridge west of the river many direct targets were successfully engaged. Meanwhile "D" Coy section advanced with Infantry. About 15:15 hours the enemy counter attacked in force but was met with determined resistance from Lewis Infantry and machine Guns. Ammunition became exhausted and after hand to hand fighting our troops were forced West of the river after inflicting heavy casualties on the enemy. The morning attack had been covered by a creeping machine gun barrage from "B" Coy Guns, which later moved forward and engaged several battle targets especially during the counter attack when they also fired an S.O.S. barrage East of the railway. The remainder of "A" Coy and of "D" Coy and the whole of "C" Coy had continued as on the 11th and in the evening the whole Battalion was relieved by the 5th Battalion and moved into billets at CAVDRY. Casualties - 2/Lt. Burton wounded, Lt. Rowe M.C. wounded (remained at duty) 4 o.r. wounded.	Appx
	13		Battalion in billets in CAVDRY. Casualties - nil.	Appx
	14		Battalion in billets in CAVDRY. Casualties - nil.	Appx
	15		Battalion in billets in CAVDRY. Casualties - nil.	Appx
	16		Battalion in billets in CAVDRY. Casualties - nil.	Appx
	17		Battalion in billets in CAVDRY. Casualties - nil.	Appx
	18		Battalion in billets in CAVDRY. One of "C" Coys billets destroyed by shell. Casualties 3 o.r. killed 8 o.r. wounded.	Appx
	19		Battalion in billets in CAVDRY. Inspected by Divisional Commander. Casualties - nil.	Appx

Army Form C. 2118.

WAR DIARY
or
INTELLIGENCE SUMMARY.
(Erase heading not required.) OCTOBER, 1918.

Place	Date	Hour	Summary of Events and Information	Remarks and references to Appendices
			Reference:- Maps - France, Sheets 57 B N.E. and 51 A S.E. 1:20000.	
	20		Battalion in billets in CAUDRY.- Casualties nil.	
	21		Battalion in billets in CAUDRY.- Casualties nil.	
	22		"D" Coy moved to BRIASTRE.- "A" Coy. moved to CLERMONT CHATEAU.- Advanced Battalion H.2. moved to CLERMONT CHATEAU. "B" and "C" Companies, with rear echelons of "A" and "D" Companies and Rear Battalion H.2. remained in CAUDRY.- Casualties	
	23		Three sections of "D" Company went forward with 111th Brigade and assisted in consolidating the line on the outskirts of NEUVILLE. One section remained in reserve in BRIASTRE. An enemy machine gun post consisting of three machine guns and about twenty men, was captured by this Company. Company H.2 and its Reserve section moved to BEAURAIN.- "A" Company moved to BEAURAIN and took up positions from which a barrage was fired. "B" Company moved to BRIASTRE.- "C" Company moved forward with 112th Brigade group to BEAURAIN.- Advanced Battalion H.2. moved to BEAURAIN, and Rear Battalion H.2. and Rear Echelons moved to BRIASTRE.- Casualties - Captain Eric Chater wounded, 2 o.r. killed and 2 wounded.	
	24		The 112th Brigade passed through the 111th Brigade, and "C" Company moved forward with the 112th Brigade. "B" Company moved forward with 63rd Brigade and took up defensive positions on X 21 and X 27 with Company H.2. in BEAVRAIN. The Reserve section of "D" Company moved up to SALESCHES Station, and at night the whole of "D" Company with others	

Army Form C. 2118.

WAR DIARY
or
INTELLIGENCE SUMMARY.
(Erase heading not required.) OCTOBER 1918.

Reference Map France Sheet 51A S.E. 1:20000.

Place	Date	Hour	Summary of Events and Information	Remarks and references to Appendices
to BEAURAIN.	24		"A" Company moved up to NEVILLE and took up positions. Advanced Battalion H.Q. moved to SALESCHES. Rear Battalion H.Q. and Rear Echelons moved to BEAURAIN.— Casualties 1 o.r. killed, 5 o.r. wounded.	
	25		"C" Company's guns remained in positions in X.3, X.9 and X.15, with Company H.Q. in SALESCHES.— "B" Company moved up to SALESCHES and took up positions along the Railway. "A" Company were in positions in X.10A, X.15b, X.16a and X.10c.— "D" Company, Rear Battalion H.Q. and Rear Echelons in BEAURAIN. Advanced Battalion H.Q. in SALESCHES. Casualties 1 o.r. wounded.	
	26		Locations as on 25th. Casualties:— Captain R.W. Peacock wounded, 1 o.r. killed and 1 o.r. wounded.	
	27		No change in locations. Harassing fire was carried out. Casualties 3 o.r. wounded.	
	28		"D" Company relieved "A" Company in the line, and "A" Company withdrew to billets in BEAURAIN.— Batteries no change in locations. Casualties 2 o.r. wounded.	
	29		No change in locations. Casualties 1 o.r. wounded.	
	30		No change in locations. Casualties nil.	
	31		No change in locations. Casualties 1 o.r. wounded.	

Lieut.-Col.
Commanding 37th Bn. Machine Gun. Corps.

37th Bn Machine Gun Corps

War Diary

for month of November 1918

Army Form C. 2118.

WAR DIARY
or
INTELLIGENCE SUMMARY.
(Erase heading not required.)

NOVEMBER, 1918.

Place	Date	Hour	Summary of Events and Information	Remarks and references to Appendices
			Reference Map FRANCE Sheet 51A S.E. 1:20,000	BPH BPH BPH BPH BPH BPH BPH BPH BPH
	1		Advanced Battalion H.Q. in SALESCHES. Rear Battalion H.Q., Rear Echelons of Companies, and "A" Coy in BEAURAIN. A raid was carried out by the 63rd Brigade, "D" Company being a batterage. Casualties - 1 o.r. wounded.	
	2		Locations as on 1st. "D" Company supported a raid made by the 63rd Brigade. Casualties - 1 o.r. wounded.	
	3		Advanced Battalion H.Q. moved to GHISSIGNIES. "A" Company moved up to SALESCHES and bivouaced for the night. Rear Battalion H.Q. and Rear Echelons in BEAURAIN. Casualties 2 o.r. wounded.	
	4		All Companies assisted in the attack by the Division on LOUVIGNIES, JOLIMETZ, and the FORÊT DE MORMAL. Rear Battalion H.Q. and rear echelons remained in BEAURAIN. Casualties - Lieut. A. Rain wounded, 4 o.r. killed and 24 o.r. wounded.	
	5		The 5th Division passed through, and the Battalion came back to billets in SALESCHES. Rear Echelons also moved to SALESCHES. Casualties - nil.	
	6		Battalion in billets in SALESCHES. Casualties nil.	
	7		No change. Casualties - nil. Training carried out.	
	8		No change. Casualties - 1 o.r. wounded accidentally. Training carried out.	
	9		No change. Training carried out. Casualties nil.	

B. Coy. Knoop Lt Col

Army Form C. 2118.

WAR DIARY
or
INTELLIGENCE SUMMARY.
(Erase heading not required.)

NOVEMBER 1918.

Place	Date	Hour	Summary of Events and Information	Remarks and references to Appendices
			Reference Maps:- France Sheet 51A. S.E. 1:20000 France Sheet 57B. 1:40.000.-	
	10		Battalion in billets in SALESCHES.- Training carried out.: Casualties - nil.-	APP
	11		Armistice signed and hostilities ceased at 11.00 hours. Battalion moved to billets in CAUDRY.- Casualties - nil.-	APP
	12 to 30		Battalion in billets in CAUDRY.- Training carried out: On the 22nd the Divisional Commander held a Review of the Division.- Casualties - nil.-	APP

Hy. Forsyth Pfs.
Lieut.-Col.
Commanding 37th Bn. Machine Gun. Corps.

37TH BN. M.G.C.

WAR DIARY for the month of December 1918.

Army Form C. 2118.

WAR DIARY
or
INTELLIGENCE SUMMARY.
(Erase heading not required.)

December, 1918

Reference:- maps 1:100000 France - sheets - VALENCIENNES 12, NAMUR 8.

Date	Hour	Summary of Events and Information	Remarks and references to Appendices
1		The Battalion moved from billets in CAUDRY to billets in NEUVILLE.	
2		The Battalion moved to billets in FRASNOY.	
3 to 13		Battalion in billets in FRASNOY. - Village cleaned up and training carried out.	
14		The Battalion moved to billets in BERMERIES.	
15		The Battalion moved to billets in SOUS LE BOIS.	
16		Battalion in billets in SOUS LE BOIS.	
17		The Battalion moved to billets in BOUSSOIS.	
18		The Battalion moved to billets in BINCHE.	
19		The Battalion moved to billets in ROUX.	
20		The Battalion moved to billets in GOSSELIES.	
21 to 31		Battalion in billets in GOSSELIES. - Training carried out.	

9812

War Diary

37 Bn Machine Gun Corps

Month of January 1919

Army Form C. 2118.

WAR DIARY
or
INTELLIGENCE SUMMARY.
(Erase heading not required.)

Instructions regarding War Diaries and Intelligence Summaries are contained in F. S. Regs., Part II. and the Staff Manual respectively. Title pages will be prepared in manuscript.

Place	Date	Hour	Summary of Events and Information	Remarks and references to Appendices
GOSSELIES.	Jan. 1-31st		In billets at GOSSELIES. Carrying out training and fatigues and demobilization. Men being demobilised as under:—	
			3 Officers 19 O.Rs.	
			Jan 9 — " 9 "	
			" 13 — " 20 "	
			" 18 — " 12 "	
			" 21 — " 8 "	
			" 22 — " 42 "	
			" 25 2 " 33 "	
			" 26 — " 58 "	
			" 28 — " 22 "	
			" 29 2 " 1 "	
			" 31 — " — "	

Step Moyfae Lt Col.
bdg 34th Bn. W.R.C.

37th Bn. Machine Gun Corps.

Army Form C. 2118.

WAR DIARY
or
INTELLIGENCE SUMMARY.

(Erase heading not required.)

37TH MACHINE GUN BATTALION.

Place	Date	Hour	Summary of Events and Information	Remarks and references to Appendices
GOSSELIES	Feb 1st to 28th 1919		In billets at GOSSELIES, BELGIUM. Carrying out demobilisation training and fatigues. Checking and storing equipment of establishment & handing in surplus equipment.	

Roy Hoyle Lieut.-Col.
Commanding 37th Bn. Machine Gun. Corps.

Army Form C. 2118.

WAR DIARY
or
INTELLIGENCE SUMMARY.
(Erase heading not required.)

Instructions regarding War Diaries and Intelligence Summaries are contained in F. S. Regs., Part II. and the Staff Manual respectively. Title pages will be prepared in manuscript.

Place	Date	Hour	Summary of Events and Information	Remarks and references to Appendices
GOSSELIES. BELGIUM.	May 1 to 31st		In billets at GOSSELIES doing fatigues, and training and carrying out demobilization	

R.P. Shepherd
Capt & Adjt Cdg
Cdg 37th M. G. Bn

39th Bn Machine Gun Corps

WAR DIARY
or
INTELLIGENCE SUMMARY.

Army Form C. 2118.

Place	Date	Hour	Summary of Events and Information	Remarks and references to Appendices
MULHEIM	May 1st to 21st		In billets at MULHEIM receiving drafts and organising the battalion and carrying out training and education.	
	May 21st to 31st		Orders received for disbandment of battalion, which was carried out by sending drafts to 9th and 29th Bn M.G.C. & cadre for the retention of nucleus of 120 O.Rs.	

J. Mair.
Major
Commanding 39th Bn. Machine Gun. Corps.